Belonging

Belonging

An Introduction to the Faith and Life of the Christian Reformed Church

Wilbert M. Van Dyk

Library of Congress Cataloging in Publication Data

Van Dyk, Wilbert M.
   Belonging: an introduction to the faith and life of
the Christian Reformed Church.

   1. Christian Reformed Church—Doctrinal and con-
troversial works, Popular. I. Title
BX6821.2.V36   285.7'31   82-1241
ISBN 0-933140-43-6 (pbk.)   AACR2

© 1982 by the Board of Publications of the Christian
   Reformed Church 2850 Kalamazoo Ave. SE, Grand
   Rapids, MI 49560.

   All rights reserved.
   Printed in the United States of America.
   ISBN 0-933140-43-6

Contents

*What is your only comfort
in life and in death?*

That I am not my own,
but belong—
   body and soul,
   in life and in death—
to my faithful Savior Jesus Christ.

Heidelberg Catechism Q & A 1

Preface

The title of this book, *Belonging,* has two interwoven meanings. The first of these is clear, for this book introduces the faith and life of the Christian Reformed Church and invites the reader to "belong" to that church. The second deeper meaning is the true condition for belonging to any church—belonging to Jesus Christ. We trust these two belongings are fully interwoven in the church we introduce here.

A church is a company of believers bound together by a common faith. That faith is expressed in worship practices, fellowship patterns, and ways of living. Ideally the church's life grows directly out of its faith; actually traditions and customs are also formative. But as far as possible this book tries to show how the life and worship characteristics of Christian Reformed people stem from what they believe and confess. So faith and life are introduced together.

This book was planned by three agencies of the Christian Reformed Church: its North American outreach agency (Board of Home Missions), its radio and TV ministry (The Back to God Hour/CRC-TV), and its church education agency (Education Department of the Board of Publications). It was written by an experienced and capable pastor—Rev. Wilbert M. Van Dyk, minister of the Plymouth Heights Christian Reformed Church, Grand Rapids, Michigan. And it is offered with the hope that the picture it gives of our church is both an honest and attractive invitation to share fully in what we believe and do together as a family of God.

Harvey A. Smit
Director of Education

Artist's Statement

The stained glass window that appears on the cover and pages of this pamphlet was constructed specifically for this publication. We chose a medium and design which best represents our church as it is today. Below is an explanation of the window.

Cover: Belonging, An Introduction to the Faith and Life of the Christian Reformed Church

Stained glass has always been a traditional medium for church decoration, but when combined with a contemporary design, it also gives a very clear picture of the Christian Reformed Church: we find our roots in the Bible, the gospel of Jesus Christ, and seek to proclaim and apply the teaching of Scripture to the world today.

Chapter 1: Who Are We?

Just as it took many steps to create the window, many people and experiences have combined to form the name of our denomination.

Chapter 2: Where Did We Come From?

As many small pieces are used to make up the window, our church is made up of a wide variety of people from many different backgrounds.

Chapter 3: What Do We Believe?

The triangle represents the Trinity. We believe there is one God who exists in three persons—Father, Son, and Holy Spirit. This belief, based on the Bible, is expressed in the creeds and confessions of our church.

Chapter 4: What Do We Believe about God, the Father?

The many blue pieces of glass, found in all parts of the window, represent God. The blue glass and the vertical lines convey our belief that God created and rules over all things.

Chapter 5: What Do We Believe about God, the Son?

The cross is a universal symbol of Christ.

Chapter 6: What Do We Believe about God, the Holy Spirit?

The bright pieces of red, yellow, and orange glass symbolize the Holy Spirit who appeared in tongues of fire on the day of Pentecost, the beginning of the church of Jesus Christ.

Chapter 7: What Do We Think of the Church?

The combination of cross and triangle points to Christ, the chief officer of the church, who rules his people by his Word and Spirit.

Chapter 8: How Do We Lead the Christian Life?

Like the leading which runs through every part of the window, the Ten Commandments shape our entire lifestyle.

Chapter 9: What Are We Doing in the World?

A stained glass window has no beauty unless light shines through it. The Christian Reformed Church seeks, through its mission programs and ministry activities, to reveal Jesus Christ, the Light of the world.

Dean R. Heetderks

Our Family Name

Chapter One

Perhaps you've noticed this name—Christian Reformed Church. You may have seen it on a church building, on a church school bus, or on a triangular road sign. You may have glimpsed it on the television screen or heard it spoken on the radio. You may have read it under the logo of a church school curriculum or, if you've been traveling a lot, you may have seen it stenciled on the back of a community developer's four-wheel-drive truck in Sierra Leone or an agriculturalist's materials in Bangladesh. In North America it's possible to find this name printed in English and French, Navaho and Zuni, Spanish and Korean, Chinese and Vietnamese—Christian Reformed Church.

What's in a Name?

Some names have no special meaning. Why call a pet dog Fido? Why give the name Toby to a pet turtle? Maybe for no reason at all; that name just seems to fit. The dog looks like a Fido and the turtle like a Toby.

But the name *Christian Reformed Church* is different. It belongs to us and identifies us. It means something. Three words make up the name and each of those words helps describe who we are.

To begin with the last word, we are a *church*. That's a word commonly used in several different ways. A church is the building around the corner. A church is the new group of people meeting in the local gym. A church is an entire denomination— the Methodist Church, the Baptist Church, or the Christian Reformed Church. Most inclusively of all, the church is *all* believers in Jesus Christ.

Yet where we come to know the church is in that certain group of people meeting in that certain building down the street. That's the sense in which the New Testament uses the word. When it speaks of church, it says literally (in the Greek word) those who are "called out." The church is people who are called out of their homes into places of public worship, called by God out of selfishness and sin to become part of a fellowship, to worship him, and to do his work on earth. That's what we are—people who have been called out. We are a *church*.

The second word in our name is *Reformed*. Sometimes people misunderstand that. They think it's the Christian "Reform" Church. To be sure, we like to think we have something to do with reforming people, but the name is *Reformed*.

That part of our name identifies us as one with the historic Christian church. Churches have used the name *Reformed* for more than 450 years. Already in the 1500s the name *Reformed* was given to a church that tried to form itself again after the pattern of the New Testament church. So to call ourselves a *Reformed* church is to put into our very name an idea that means a great deal to us. It means we belong to the whole history of the Christian church.

We like to sing the old songs "Faith of Our Fathers" and "Onward, Christian Soldiers." The word *Reformed* captures that sense of belonging to the great church of Christ. We're not a sect or a cult—here today, gone tomorrow. We're not a strange-looking page in the book of church history. To say that we're *Reformed* says at least this much: we belong to the whole historic development of the church of Jesus Christ.

The most important part of our name is the first word, *Christian.* An old story tells of a soldier in the army of Alexander the

Great whose name was also Alexander. One day the soldier Alexander was brought into the presence of Emperor Alexander and accused of cowardly behavior on the battlefield. The emperor commanded the soldier, "Either get to the front lines and fight or change your name. For sir," said the emperor, "you bear a great name." That's how we feel about that name *Christian*. It's a great name. It identifies us with the Lord Jesus Christ. It means we belong to him and are his followers.

The *Christian Reformed Church*. That's our name: followers of Jesus Christ in a long historic tradition of people whom God has called out to be in fellowship with him and with each other. There are times when that name scares us. It claims so much. We're not always everything that the name says we are. But confessing our failures, we still make bold to introduce ourselves.

The Church as Family

If you ask what one word best describes how we of the Christian Reformed Church think of ourselves, that word is probably *family.* The idea of the church as family is a familiar one in the Bible. Both prophets and apostles used family imagery to portray the people of God—in three special ways.

First, the Bible depicts God as the husband of the church. The Old Testament prophet Isaiah uses this image in chapter 54:5: "For your Maker is your husband, the Lord of hosts is his name." The prophets Jeremiah and Hosea also spoke of God's relationship to his people as that of a husband to a wife. And centuries later the apostle Paul wrote to the Christian church at Ephesus. In chapter 5 of that letter he described the relationship between Christ and the church. He said it is like a marriage in which Christ is the husband and the church is the wife.

This recurring marriage image tells us that God and his people, Christ and his church, are bound together by faithful vows. There's a covenant, a sealed promise between them that ties them inseparably to each other. It's a powerfully attractive picture to us because it speaks of mutual faithfulness and love. True, not every marriage is like that. Some are tragic. Some are marred by faithlessness. But the marriage between God and his church is a beautiful picture of *family* at its best. And that's how we see ourselves: the imperfect wife of a perfect husband who loves us and welcomes our love for him.

The second way in which the Bible describes the church as a family is probably the most familiar. God is our Father. That makes us, the church, his children who look to him for love, care, and instruction. Complementing that image, the Bible also says God is like a mother to us. Isaiah wrote that as a word of assurance in his prophecy. "For thus says the Lord: '. . . As one whom his mother comforts, so I will comfort you' " (Isa. 66:12–13).

Still the more common biblical image is of God our Father. That's certainly how Jesus taught us to begin the prayer we've come to know as the Lord's Prayer. "Pray then like this," said Jesus in words recorded in Matthew 6:9, "Our Father who art in heaven. . . ."

To think of God as our Father in heaven is very important to the Christian Reformed Church: it means that God is the one who lovingly controls every part of life and that we are the children of the heavenly Father. Both sides of that relationship teach us to think of ourselves as living under the authority, love, and care of the God to whom we bring our childlike trust and obedience.

The third way in which the Bible describes the church as a family is in terms of brothers and sisters. Although we don't usually call each other "Sister Sarah" or "Brother John," that's how we think of ourselves: as brothers and sisters in one family. We're brothers and sisters, of course, because we have the same heavenly Father. That Father sent his eternal Son into our world so that, through our faith in Jesus Christ, we might become children of God and therefore brothers and sisters in the family of the Christian faith.

Often the vision we have of ourselves is like a mold that forms the way we live. A person who sees himself as "king of the mountain" will probably try to live as if he's on top of the world. How we think of ourselves shapes us. It forms us. It molds us. And because the Christian Reformed Church thinks of itself as God's family, it lives and worships as a family. Because we think of each other as brothers and sisters in the Christian faith, we act towards each other as we do.

This makes an interesting picture. As anyone who has brothers and sisters knows, siblings can sometimes fight the hardest, say the nastiest things to each other, and squabble over all kinds of small details. They also take each other for granted. We're embarrassed about it, but as a church that kind of thing happens among us too—family squabbles and taking each other for granted.

But it's also true, as anyone who has a brother or sister knows, that "blood is thicker than water." When one member of the family is threatened or hurt or in trouble, all the members draw closer together and help each other. As a church we're a family bound together by the water of baptism. That water, the symbol of Christ's cleansing blood, makes us one family. And contrary to the old saying, in this case water is *thicker* than blood.

Living as a Family

Because we think of ourselves as a new, stronger family—as brothers and sisters in Jesus Christ—we show a family concern for each other. Wherever possible we provide Christian day schools, both for our own and each other's children. We support Christian rest and retirement homes and Christian hospitals for each other's old and sick. Our deacons help the poor among us. We develop programs to assist the physically, mentally, and emotionally handicapped. You'll find us visiting the sick, bringing meals to shut-ins, weeping with those who sorrow, rejoicing with those who celebrate. We try to bear each other's burdens, increase each other's joys, and enrich each other's lives. After all, we're a family. We're brothers and sisters.

Thinking of ourselves as children of God affects the way we live in the world. Christian Reformed people like to talk about a "kingdom perspective" or "a world and life view." We resist the notion that God is interested only in our souls not our bodies, that God cares only about our worship not our work and play, that God rules only spiritual things and leaves material things to us to decide. We don't think of our religion as a box marked "to be opened only on Sunday." We believe that God is the Lord of the whole universe and the Master of every moment and movement of life. Children, we remember, are not children of their parents only at mealtime or at bedtime. They are children of their parents twenty-four hours a day, seven days a week, for as long as they live. Similarly, we're children of God in every part of life.

Because that fatherhood of God is such an overarching reality in the Christian Reformed Church, it's not surprising that Christian Reformed people dedicate not only their churches but also their businesses to God's glory and service. It's not surprising to hear Christian Reformed people speak with as much conviction about the Christian's duty in politics, economics, and social problems as they speak about the obligation to worship and witness. It's not surprising that Christian Reformed mission workers not only preach the gospel, but also provide blankets and carpenters for those whose homes have been destroyed by storm or earthquake. To think of God as our Father and of ourselves as his children translates into a life that is lived under the authority of God and in the embrace of his love.

Our identity comes into sharpest focus in the Sunday worship services. Worship is often a person's first real introduction to the Christian Reformed Church. It can be an impressive experience. The people gathered in the church seem to care about each other as brothers and sisters should. The bulletin of the day probably says something about congregational life and the joys and sorrows of particular members. The atmosphere of the worship service is reverent. The choir sings with real conviction, "Surely God is in this place." The songs, the prayers, the sermon, the sacraments, even the announcements— all are expressions of a church that sees itself as a family of God. There is, of course, much variation in the way different Christian Reformed churches worship, but common to most of them will be the vision of what the church is—children of God, brothers and sisters in Jesus Christ.

And our family continues to grow. Why? Because we're incomplete; we need others. We don't need them simply to fill empty spaces in our pews, or to pay unpaid bills, or to add numbers to growth statistics. We need others because of who we are and what we have. That's a treasure meant to be shared. We need others because our joy is not complete until others have come to share it with us. Like anything else that excites us—a beautiful vacation trip, a family graduation, or a new car—our joy is not really full until it's spilled over onto someone else; our satisfaction isn't complete until others have shared in the family of God.

That's why we introduce ourselves—to explain to others who we are in the hope that they will be attracted to join us in this family experience called the Christian Reformed Church.

Our
Origins

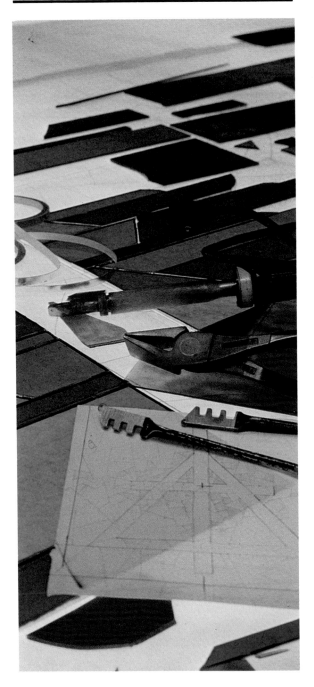

Chapter Two

Klaas and his cousin Henk sat at the edge of the dike in North Holland watching the boat traffic sail up and down the canal and talking quietly. They were troubled. Something was wrong; something was up in the air. This Sunday afternoon their fathers and uncles had all gathered for a serious talk after church. Klaas and Henk, drinking tea in the corner of the room, had overheard phrases like ". . . as it used to be," "if the government insists on our . . .," ". . . freedom to obey the Bible," and a new, exciting one, ". . . move to America." Henk and Klaas couldn't put it all together, but they knew something was in the wind, that it concerned the church, and that a big decision was being made. What Klaas and Henk and even their parents didn't know was that the seeds were being sown for what would eventually become the Christian Reformed Church in North America.

Here's how it all began. In the early 1800s the king of the Netherlands introduced a new church constitution that gave him far greater control over church affairs. He used that new authority to bring in some liberalizing changes that resulted in growing indifference to the historic creeds—changes like a new hymnal, *Evangelical Hymns.* A small group of Christians objected to those changes. But they were not powerful people. Most were poor and lacked the influence needed to stop government interference in church affairs. So finally they took the only action left to them: they started a new church.

This was not a popular action. Both the old church and the government were angry. The king ordered this new church to cease its separate worship services and sent soldiers to enforce those orders. When this small group defied the government and met anyway, neighbors mocked them and made so much noise that often meetings had to be canceled.

About this same time the people in the Netherlands were hearing attractive reports about North America—that it was a country with plenty of job opportunities, chance for advancement, lots of cheap land, and freedom to worship God without government interference. To the leaders of this new, persecuted church it seemed that God was opening a door and inviting them to enter. In the brand-new country of America they might find a brand-new beginning, free of the difficulties they were experiencing in Holland. The more they thought and talked, the more obvious it seemed—they must move to America. So move they did. A small, courageous group of men, women, and children packed their bags, boarded a boat, and sailed west. One band settled in western Michigan, another in south-central Iowa.

These new settlers from Holland joined the Dutch Reformed Church in America. It was a natural move. Dutch settlers had come to America in the early 1600s and had established a Reformed Church in New York as early as 1628. If the settlers of two centuries later and the existing Reformed Church had been happy with each other, the Christian Reformed Church might never have come into being. But things didn't go well.

After a time the new settlers in western Michigan began to hear disturbing reports about the Reformed Church. They heard that some of the ministers didn't preach the old, solid Reformed doctrines, that most

Reformed churches sang hymns in addition to the old biblical psalms, that almost anybody was welcomed to the Lord's supper, and that some members of the Reformed Church were also members of the Masonic Lodge. These were the very issues over which they had separated from the old church in the Netherlands. Did the Reformed Church in America follow these same erroneous ways?

Actually, some of those reports may have become distorted in traveling the many miles from New York, where the Reformed Church was largely concentrated, to western Michigan. But the new immigrants heard the reports and believed them. So in April of 1857 several of the new settlers decided to separate from the Reformed Church and establish a new denomination of their own in America. The Christian Reformed Church was born. It was a small beginning: four churches, some seven hundred people, and only two ministers (one whose only transportation was an ox cart). But God blessed that small beginning and the new denomination grew.

A "Dutch" Church?

At first our growth was largely due to families like those of Klaas and Henk, people immigrating from the Netherlands. In fact, for the first half century or more the language of the Christian Reformed Church was an immigrant tongue—Dutch. Even today the biggest block of names on the membership roles of most Christian Reformed churches reveals our Dutch origin—names like Bandstra, De Vries, Holland, Vander Laan, and Zylstra. Our radio preachers, administrators, pastors, professors, and church members have an astonishing variety of uncommon, hard-to-pronounce names, from Bruinooge to Van Voorthuysen.

This almost overpowering presence of Dutch family names in our church became even more marked after World War II, when a new massive influx of immigrants from the Netherlands settled in Canada. Between the late forties and the late fifties, the number of Christian Reformed Church families in Canada alone increased some sixteen times—from under 500 to more than 8,000.

One point should be clear. We're proud of our roots in the Netherlands, but we don't want to be labeled the "Dutch" church. The reason is simple: that's not what we are, so it's not how we should be known. Throughout our history we've tried to take seriously Christ's command to preach the gospel to all kinds of people. And especially during the last few decades the membership of the Christian Reformed Church has been enriched by increasing numbers of people from other national, racial, and ethnic backgrounds. To paint a fair picture of the Christian Reformed Church today, the mural would have to include Spanish- and Korean-speaking congregations and native American, black, and Vietnamese congregations. The story of the Christian Reformed Church today must include chapters not only about Klaas and Henk but also about John and Jane, Maria and Carlos, Ung Van and Hoa Thi, Latonya and Tasha, Paul and Scott. And that, of course, is exactly what Jesus Christ wants his church to be: a fellowship of people called out from all the nations of the world to follow him and do his work in the world.

Where will we be ten years from now? Fifty years? A hundred? Only God knows the future. And he has chosen not to tell us the joys and sorrows, the successes and failures it holds. That's good. If we knew the future of our church, we might be tempted to despair because of the troubles yet to be endured or to be proud because of victories yet to come. The future belongs to God. But that same God who holds the future also holds us in his hands. We walk by faith, seeking to follow where he leads.

Our Real Roots

But back to our origins. An old bit of Jewish folklore relates that two guardian angels accompany each of us through life. The one angel guards the future and opens its doors. The other angel guards the past, preserving its treasures.

We can apply that bit of wisdom to the church. The treasures of the past are our history. A right understanding of that past shows us the foundations on which our present is built; it also provides the treasures out of which God calls us into our future.

Perhaps the most important single point about our history is the intent of those Dutch settlers in western Michigan who organized a new church in 1857. They didn't mean to start something new and different. Instead they wanted to recover the past, to bring to reality what they believed Jesus Christ has always wanted his church to be and what his church had always been. In a sense the church organized in 1857 was just a continuing part of the church born on that Pentecost in Jerusalem centuries earlier.

Acts 2 tells the story of the church's birthday. Jesus Christ had been crucified and buried. The third day he rose from the dead and forty days later left his disciples and ascended into heaven. On that Pentecost the disciples were gathered, wondering how they could possibly carry on the work Jesus had told them to do. Suddenly they became aware of a mighty spiritual presence. The Holy Spirit promised by Jesus had come. And in the strength of that Spirit the disciples were able to establish the church of Jesus Christ in the world.

It's helpful to think of the church as a tree. The early church formed a single, solid trunk. Branches had not yet appeared. Certainly those early Christians also disagreed on a number of issues, but the church was one living body, united against the enormous pressures of persecution from outside. Not until the year 1054 did that single trunk fork and then split into two; the churches located in the eastern area of the Mediterranean divided from those located in the western area of that inland sea. In climbing the tree of church history we follow the western branch, the church headquartered in Rome.

The church of Rome was large and powerful. But over the years the story of that church had turned sad and sour. Church officials had been corrupted by wealth and power. Church members had lost interest in what the Bible taught. Popes had excommunicated emperors and emperors had deposed popes. Bribery, ritual, formalism, and selfishness had made the church a mockery, a tragic shadow of what Jesus had wanted it to be.

Out of what seemed a dying branch, the Protestant Reformation formed as a new, vibrantly alive limb of the church's tree. The year was 1517; the day, October 31. A man named Martin Luther had been reading and studying the Bible. Based on what the Bible said, he concluded that the church of his day was going terribly wrong. According to the popular account, on October 31, 1517, he spoke his mind publicly by nailing to the cathedral door at Wittenburg, Germany, ninety-five statements of faith which he believed were true to Scripture. These were neither new rules for church government nor new revolutionary teachings—they were simply statements calling the church back to the Bible's teaching. The great church of Rome refused to listen and change its ways (it wasn't until some decades later that the Roman Church reformed itself and new life flowed through the old branch), so a new church began. People who followed Luther's teachings became known as Lutherans. They are one cluster of branches on the tree of church history.

About the same time another branch was beginning to grow on that tree. A man called John Calvin, educated first for a career as a priest, then as lawyer, turned into another reformer of the church. John Calvin became convinced that the church had to return to the teachings of Scripture. The Bible teaches, Calvin wrote, that God is the sovereign Lord over all, that the purpose of our existence is to praise him, and that the blessing of our existence is to enjoy him. The church is a body living under its head, the Lord Jesus Christ. Calvin's restless pen wrote on and on, exploring and explaining what the Bible teaches for the faith and life of the church.

Many came from all over Europe to learn from John Calvin. John Knox was one of these. He carried Calvin's teachings to Scotland and established churches there that became known as Presbyterian. Other followers of Calvin's teachings established churches in continental Europe; these were called Reformed. Churches who include the word *presbyterian* in their name and churches who include the word *reformed* in their name belong to the same large branch of church history. Out of that branch—more particularly out of the part of that branch that grew in the Netherlands—the Christian Reformed Church sprouted. When in the mid-1800s that little band of Christian people set out from the Netherlands, they were like a little twig branching out from the Reformed limb of the tree of church history.

Reformed and Reforming

All this talk about our origins isn't mere talk. It's very important to us to be able to trace our history as a church back to the Protestant Reformation and on down the tree of church history to the birth of the Christian church on Pentecost Sunday. It's important to us because the church of Jesus Christ in the world is really one church. We're brothers and sisters of all others who confess Jesus Christ as Savior and Lord.

We all wear denominational labels. Those labels are part of our history. We can't avoid them. But sometimes they become barriers to the Christian unity we could be enjoying. It's like the little girl whose mother was talking over the backyard hedge to a neighbor. They were discussing the possibility of the family joining a new denomination. "Mother," asked the girl (obviously not understanding the big word), "what abomination do we belong to now?" Denominations *are* abominations when they prevent us from understanding the common history that we enjoy as branches of a single tree through which the life of Jesus Christ flows. Christian Reformed Church origins locate us as part of the worldwide church, born on Pentecost Sunday, which will continue until Jesus comes again.

Yet, recognizing that unity and rejoicing in it, we also understand our distinctiveness. We are a *Christian* church that is *Reformed.* And that means, in the tradition of the Protestant Reformation, that we must be a church that places itself—in worship, work, life, and mission—under the authority of the Word and Spirit of God. That is and must remain an essential mark of the Christian Reformed Church. We cannot compromise that allegiance to the will of God.

That also makes us not just a once-reformed but a continually reforming church. The more faithful we are to God's Word and the more eager to follow God's Spirit, the more willing we become to change our ways of thinking and doing so as to fit into God's purposes for us. On the one hand, that means that some things we believe and practice do *not* change; on those things God's will is clear. But on the other hand, in those areas where God's will is unclear, the Christian Reformed Church is not locked into molds of unchanging human opinions. We have minds that search for ways to be increasingly fashioned by God's will. Committees to study the Bible's teaching about some issue are part of our church's landscape. That may seem like busy work to some, to people who don't understand what being Reformed means. But, like other churches in the Protestant Reformation tradition, we delight in the constant challenge to be reshaped as God's Spirit leads us to a better understanding of his Word.

That's so hard at times. Old familiar ways are comfortable. It's easier to drift with tradition than to take seriously the task of always reforming. But if we drift we become like the Russian soldiers of Czar Nicholas. One day the czar found a soldier guarding a weed patch and asked why he stood there. The guard replied, "Because the captain told me to." When the captain was asked why, he said, "Because it's the law." And sure enough. Old records showed that years before Catherine the Great had planted a rose bush on that spot and ordered a guard posted to protect the young bush. The rose bush had long since died, but the tradition of posting the guard had remained.

Sometimes we too guard our weed patches. "We've always done it that way," seems a convincing argument. But we really know better. We know that as a part of the Reformed branch of the tree of church history, we are a church constantly being molded, shaped, reformed into the living body of Jesus Christ according to the will of God.

Call us a Dutch church, an American church, a multiethnic church, a biracial church, a multinational church, or a historic church. All those names describe what we've been or are. But, most important, call us the Christian Reformed Church—a church that has been formed and is being formed by God's Word and Spirit.

Our Standard–
The Word of God

Chapter Three

If our name tells how we see ourselves and our origins tell what we were and hope to become, the most important part is still left untold—the standard of our faith and life. Casual conversations with fellow plane travelers usually include questions about name, home, and destination. But of possible lifelong spiritual companions we'd ask much more. We'd want to know what star they steer by, what light guides their way, what standard controls their thinking and acting.

The standard of faith and life for the group of pilgrims called the Christian Reformed Church is the Bible, the Word of God.

That's easy to say; it's harder to show. Walk into a typical Christian Reformed Church and you probably won't see fellow worshipers carrying well-worn, obviously well-read Bibles in their hands. You may hear reference to creeds as "our standards of unity." You may even find the pastor reading a Lord's Day with several questions and answers from the Catechism as the basis for his sermon. All that doesn't seem to jibe with claiming God's Word as our standard.

The Centrality of the Bible

But the Bible *does* occupy the central place in the life and faith of the Christian Reformed Church. That's demonstrated in at least five ways.

In our worship: Not only is the Bible prominent and symbolically central on each pulpit, but enough Bibles for the entire congregation are usually found in pew racks. Worshipers don't carry their own Bibles because they expect copies to be readily available for them in the church.

But more important than the number of Bibles in the church building is the centrality of Scripture in the worship service itself. From the opening greeting to the parting blessing, God is speaking to us in his Word, and our worshipful response echoes that Word. When the pastor reads the Law of God or a psalm of praise, he is reading from God's Word. When the people respond in unison, it is usually words from Scripture they say together. They sing God's Word too. Next to the Bible in the pew racks is a book called the *Psalter Hymnal.* The first 310 songs in that book use words taken directly from Scripture; they are psalms set to music. And the remaining hymns are steeped in scriptural language. When the congregation celebrates the sacraments, the language is again biblical. The minister gives a scriptural explanation of what's taking place. Finally, there's the sermon—the centerpiece of the worship service. In Christian Reformed churches the sermon is expected to be a careful exposition of God's Word, presenting Jesus Christ as God's answer to our human needs.

Take away God's Word and there's little left to our worship services. The Bible is central to our worship of God.

In our confessions: In the *Psalter Hymnal,* our denominationally produced book of praise, you'll find a hundred-page section entitled "Doctrinal Standards of the Christian Reformed Church." The existence of such standards may seem to clash with the statement that God's Word is our standard. But a close look at the contents of this section will show the opposite.

The first group of confessions is called the Ecumenical Creeds. These include the familiar Apostles' and Nicene Creeds, shared by almost every other Christian church.

These ecumenical creeds express the central biblical teaching that God is triune. God is one God who exists in three persons—Father, Son, and Holy Spirit. In the mystery of divine mathematics God the Father, God the Son, and God the Holy Spirit are still one God, none less God than the others. That's what God teaches about himself in his Word, so that's what we confess.

The other three doctrinal standards are longer outlines of what the Christian Reformed Church believes the Bible teaches. The most popular of these is called the Heidelberg Catechism. Written when the Protestant Reformation was still young, this document provides a systematic explanation of biblical truth. It's made up of 129 questions and answers, divided into 52 Lord's Days—one for each Sunday of the year. Biblical references are added to most of these questions and answers to show where in God's Word that particular teaching is found. The Christian Reformed Church requires its pastors to follow the outline of the Heidelberg Catechism in their preaching. That way, congregations hear a balanced diet of biblical preaching rather than a smorgasbord of the minister's favorite texts.

The other two doctrinal standards are the Belgic Confession and the Canons of Dort. The Confession was written in 1561 to demonstrate that the teachings of Reformed churches were and are true to Scripture. The Canons (*canon* means "a rule") are more difficult. These rules of faith were adopted at the great synod held in the city of Dordrecht in the Netherlands in 1618–19. They define the Reformed understanding of what the Bible teaches about God's electing love, our total sinfulness, and God's way of drawing us into fellowship with him through Jesus Christ by the power of the Holy Spirit.

In our education: We of the Reformed tradition are sometimes criticized for emphasizing the head more than the heart. If that's true, the solution is not to emphasize the head less, but the heart more. Qualities of heart and mind are both valuable and important for understanding God's Word. The Christian Reformed Church has always hungered for biblical knowledge and our education programs show that.

Christian Reformed churches usually offer a wide range of opportunities to learn more about God's Word. Bible study societies for men, women, children, young people, and senior citizens are woven into the fabric of congregational life. A church calendar may include a Bible study breakfast, a Coffee Break Bible study, and a Sunday morning or weekday evening Bible study group meeting. That's not for show. It indicates the Christian Reformed Church's commitment to knowing God's Word.

The name of our denominational church school materials reveals the same accent. Called BIBLE WAY, this curriculum provides study materials for preschoolers through adults. BIBLE WAY courses reflect the Church Order requirement that children and young people receive instruction "in the teaching of the Scriptures as formulated in the creeds of the church, in order to prepare them to profess their faith publicly and to assume their Christian responsibilities in the church and in the world."

Our education program is one of our distinguishing features; what makes it distinctive is its wholehearted commitment to God's Word.

In our mission: Some churches study the Bible only to enrich themselves. They become fat in Bible study. That's a sin which should be repented of. To read the Bible as if it is only for our own benefit is to read it wrongly. God's Word is indeed intended to prosper our own faith life, but it also demands we tell the good news to the world. The seriousness with which a church takes Scripture can be measured by its willingness to carry out Christ's mission in the world.

The Bible tells us to go into all the world and witness, to give the cup of cold water in Christ's name. In the language of the Heidelberg Catechism, we must "proclaim and publicly declare the gospel" so that the kingdom of heaven might be opened to those who believe. And the Canons of Dort insist that the world hear the gospel call so that God may gather his people eternally to himself.

Does the barometer of our mission work show a sufficient obedience to this scriptural call to go, speak, and do in the name of Christ? We could undoubtedly do more, but at least the barometer is rising. Increasingly local congregations are exploring ways of Christian outreach. And our denomination continues to expand radio broadcasting, mission work at home and abroad, and a worldwide relief effort. The mission of our church seems to show an allegiance to God's Word.

In our homes: An evidence of the centrality of the Bible that doesn't show in our public worship gatherings is our personal and family devotions. Devotions are not required by the church; neither does anyone have to give an account of them. Still much personal and family time is spent with the Bible. It's a deeply ingrained habit for most Christian Reformed people.

Some of our church people read the Bible first thing in the morning, others last thing at night. Almost all have either personal or family worship at mealtime. This usually involves both Bible reading and prayer. We pray because we can't properly listen to God speak to us in his Word unless we open our hearts to him in prayer. Prayer and Bible reading, Bible reading and prayer; ideally we should spend as much time with one as with the other. Both are needed to maintain good conversation with God. And ideally there should be no time limits. We should live prayerfully as people of the Word. Each step of the journey of life ought to be taken in prayer that recognizes our dependence on God, and with a Spirit-created willingness to be formed and molded by what God reveals in his Word about himself and his will for us.

Our worship, our confessions, our education, our mission, and our home—all feature the centrality of God's Word, the Bible. That Word of God is the standard of our thinking and living.

What We Believe about the Bible
Why is the Bible so central to our faith as a church? Because we believe it to be God's Word, one of the ways God shows himself to us. According to the Belgic Confession, God uses two means to make himself known to us. The first of these is his creation, preservation, and government of the universe—"a most elegant book, leading us to see clearly the invisible things of God." A delicate flower, a towering mountain, a twinkling star, a scurrying ant—all are the word of God to us. "The heavens are telling the glory of God; and the firmament proclaims his handiwork" (Ps. 19:1).

But because of our natural human sinfulness, because we've become "futile in our thinking and our senseless minds were darkened" (Rom. 1:21), we need another word from the Lord. We can no longer learn about God from the book of nature as we ought. So God has given us a second "most elegant book," the Bible. John Calvin called this second book the needed spectacles, the eyeglasses that correct our vision, bringing everything into focus and letting us read God's presence and work in our world.

When we put on these spectacles of the Bible, the truth that comes into sharpest focus is Jesus Christ. He is the one in whom God makes himself most clearly known to us. In the first chapter of his Gospel the apostle John describes Jesus as "the Word of God." Later, according to the story told in John, Philip asked Jesus, "Lord, show us the Father." Jesus replied, "He who has seen me has seen the Father" (14:8, 9) because as Jesus had said earlier, "I and the Father are one" (10:30). The only way we come to know God and his saving love is in Jesus Christ. For Jesus is the Word of God.

We also call the Bible the Word of God, but never in the same sense as Jesus. Jesus is the *eternal* Word of God. If it were possible to destroy Jesus, by that act the Word of God would be destroyed. God would have nothing more to say to us. But that's not true of the Bible. Throughout history people who hate Christians have attempted to stamp out Christianity by destroying all Bibles. But even if they had succeeded, they would not have destroyed the Word of God.

Jesus as God's Word and the Bible as God's Word are something like our personal word to a friend in a letter we might write. The letter is truly our word. But even if the letter is destroyed, our word isn't destroyed. Or it's like a phonograph record. You go into a store and the clerk says, "This is Beethoven's Ninth." And it is. But if the record is broken, that doesn't break Beethoven's Ninth Symphony. That's the kind of difference there is between Jesus as God's Word and the Bible as God's Word.

Jesus is God's Word and we worship him. The Bible is God's Word but we never worship it. The Bible always directs our thoughts beyond itself to Jesus, the one in whom God reveals himself to us. Jesus, however, calls our attention to himself as the Father's gift of love for our salvation. That's precisely what John said at the conclusion of his Gospel: "These [things] are written that you may believe that Jesus is the Christ, the Son of God, and that believing you may have life in his name" (20:31).

All our reading, studying, discussing, and preaching the Bible directs us to God's plan for our salvation in Jesus Christ. This is sometimes called the redemptive-historical method of studying Scripture. We view each passage in the light of God's program of salvation. The Genesis record of our beginnings; the long, often painful story of the people of Israel; the brief life and brutal death of Jesus of Nazareth; the glorious seeding of the early church by God's Spirit; the victorious promises of God for the present and future—all these are best understood in the light of the Bible's great and central theme: Jesus Christ is Savior and Lord. We don't claim that every church school lesson, every meditation, every sermon must reflect only this truth, but we do believe that God's written Word, the Bible, shows us God's living Word, Jesus Christ.

And God himself breathed out that written Word. As the apostle Peter wrote, "No prophecy of scripture is a matter of one's own interpretation, because no prophecy ever came by the impulse of man, but men moved by the Holy Spirit spoke from God"

(2 Pet. 1:20–21). This is called inspiration. It means that God himself moved the authors of the Bible to write exactly what he wanted them to write so that he could accomplish precisely what he wanted to accomplish. Paul says it quite plainly: "All scripture is inspired by God and profitable for teaching, for reproof, for correction, and for training in righteousness, that the man of God may be complete, equipped for every good work" (2 Tim. 3:16–17). God's authorship makes the Bible a book quite different from any other.

There's an old story about a minister packing his suitcase for a weekend preaching assignment. With everything packed, he still had a small corner left. "In that spot," he told his young daughter, "I'll pack a guidebook, a lamp, a mirror, a telescope, a book of poems, a number of biographies, a bundle of old letters, a hymnal, and a sharp sword." "But Daddy," she said, "You'll never get it all in." "Yes, I will," he replied, reaching for his Bible. "The Bible is all of those and more." The point is clear: the Bible is in a class by itself.

The evidence of the Bible's uniqueness is overwhelming. It was written over a span of more than a thousand years by more than thirty authors yet has a single message of God's grace for his rebellious people. Its detailed prophecies spoken a millennia earlier were accurately fulfilled in Christ's birth, life, and death. In spite of repeated attacks, the Bible has profoundly influenced millions down the centuries. Yet even all this evidence can't convince us that the Bible is God's Word. It takes the Holy Spirit's testimony. The God whose Spirit inspired the authors to write the Bible as they did is the God whose same Spirit must open our eyes to see, our ears to hear, and our hearts to receive its message. The Christian Reformed Church won't try to argue people into believing the Bible, but we pray that as we preach it and teach it, the Holy Spirit will prompt those who hear to respond in faith. Only by believing can we discover the exciting world of God's grace which the Bible reveals.

With this understanding of the Bible, the Christian Reformed Church avoids both the one extreme of those who worship this book as if it were itself God with us and the other extreme of those who dismiss it as a mere record of ancient thinking about religion. We receive the Bible with thanks to the God who gave us this revelation of himself and his plan for our salvation. We believe this revelation is inspired, error-free, authoritative, and clear enough so that through it the Holy Spirit shows us Jesus Christ, the Light of life.

During the French Revolution, a group of prisoners huddled in a crowded dark cell. One prisoner had a few fragments of the Bible. Each day, for just a brief time, a shaft of light from outside penetrated the cell's darkness. Other prisoners took turns lifting the one on their shoulders so that, in the light, he could read to them from the Scriptures. The light shone across the pages of God's Word, and the light of God's Word shone into those waiting hearts. That's how the Bible becomes the light to our paths too (Ps. 119:105) because upon it, through it, and out of it shines the Light of the world, Jesus Christ.

We Believe in God the Father

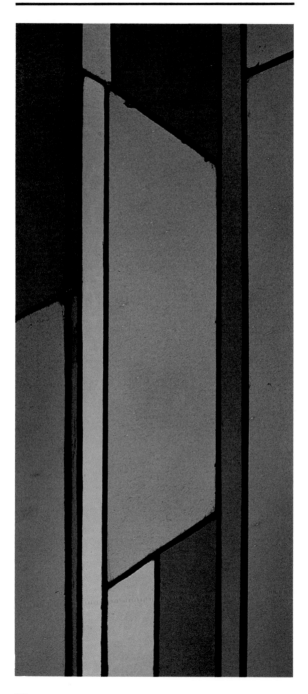

Chapter Four

Dinner table conversation that evening had been a rather depressing catalog of family problems and world crises. It made an obvious impression on the family four-year-old. Before going to bed he knelt, folded his hands, and prayed, "Dear God, take care of Mommy and Daddy and Grandma; and please, God, take good care of yourself because if anything happens to you, we're all sunk."

That prayer expresses something of the Christian Reformed Church's belief about God. As the familiar song says, "He's got the whole world in his hands." He made it, directs it, and cares for it. The whole world depends on him.

Our God is very great. He is bigger than the span of our lives. He is bigger than our communities, our nations, our world. He is bigger than the solar system, the galaxy of which it is a part, and the galaxies that lie beyond. He is bigger than our ability to picture him, bigger than the words we use to describe him. He is so big that he is present in each part of the universe at the same time. He is so big that he knows everything about everything. He is so big that no problem is too big for him to handle and no detail is too small for him to notice. When we think about God, we end by confessing with King David, "Great is the Lord, and greatly to be praised, and his greatness is unsearchable" (Ps. 145:3).

Our confession of God's greatness includes his triunity. God is not many. He is one. We echo the famous *shema* of Old Testament faith, "Hear, O Israel: The Lord our God is one Lord" (Deut. 6:4) and the New Testament creed, "There is no God but one" (1 Cor. 8:4). Yet we also believe that the one God reveals himself in three persons—Father, Son, and Holy Spirit. The story in Matthew 3 testifies to that three-ness. When Jesus, "God with us," went down into the Jordan River to be baptized, the Holy Spirit came upon him in the form of a dove and the Father spoke from heaven: "This is my beloved Son." All three persons were present. The three persons are mentioned again in Matthew 28:19, where Jesus tells his followers to "go therefore and make disciples of all nations, baptizing them in the name of the Father and of the Son and of the Holy Spirit." And Paul ends his second letter to the church at Corinth with the blessing of that triune God: "The grace of the Lord Jesus Christ and the love of God and the fellowship of the Holy Spirit be with you all."

This is a mystery of God's greatness. He is three persons, yet one God. This is how he has made himself known to us. And because God reveals himself to us as one-in-three-ness or three-in-oneness, it is possible to learn about him first as God the Father, then as God the Son, and finally as God the Holy Spirit. That kind of study begins in this chapter and continues in the next two.

The Sovereign Lord

Churches in the Reformed–Presbyterian tradition have often been stereotyped as a group with fatalistic faith in a tyrannical God. Terms like *sovereign, election,* and *predestination* are thought to betray such an idea. What does that stereotype imply? That we of the Christian Reformed Church view God as a harsh, arbitrary judge sitting in the heavens and moving people like pawns on the chessboard of life, sacrificing them easily as part of his mysterious game plan, and that we view humans as passive accepters of the divine whim to save or slay, to accept or reject, to give life or death.

That's a caricature, but it may be a believable one to many people. For the Christian Reformed Church does confess a God who is sovereign Lord of the universe, creator and ruler of it all. It does believe that we human creatures must be subject to God's almighty will. But it doesn't hold a fatalistic, sit-with-folded-hands-waiting-for-what-God-may-do-next view of life. We are not pawns in some arbitrary divine game; we are the children of God our heavenly Father.

God first reveals himself to us as Father in the biblical story of creation. In the beginning there was only God. But then God decided to "father" a universe. He brought it into being out of nothing except his determination to create. He spoke, and it was according to his word. He said, "Let there be light," and there was light. And then he created the firmament and the dry land; the sun, moon, and stars; the fish, birds, and animals; and finally his crowning achievement, human beings. God is Father of all created things.

But he is also the eternal Father. Even before the time of creation, God planned his universe. As an architect draws plans for an entire building project before the first shovel of dirt is turned, so God planned his universe and its history. This is called *predestination.*

Predestination includes both God's knowledge and his decision. God not only *knew* in advance exactly how he would create the world and how its history would develop, but he also decided that it would all come out as it has. "For those whom he foreknew he also predestined" (Rom. 8:29). "In thy book were written, every one of them, the days that were formed for me, when as yet there was none of them" (Ps. 139:16). On the basis of these and other Scripture

49

references the Christian Reformed Church believes that, from eternity, God decided to fashion a world and to direct its history according to his wonderful purposes. We believe that part of God's eternal plan was the election of some people to be saved to everlasting life. Before the foundations of the world, God chose some to be his children in Jesus Christ (Eph. 1:4, 1 Pet. 1:2).

It's extremely difficult to get our minds around this truth of God's eternal fatherhood. We can't shake the natural human pride that wants to claim that we are the masters of our own fates, the captains of our own souls. Nor can we shake the Bible's assertion that we must believe in order to be saved.

And we do have responsibilities. We aren't mere pawns. We must make decisions about family, church, home, school, business, recreation, and retirement. We rightly act as if these are our decisions to make. We rightly believe and live as if our salvation and a God-pleasing life are up to us. We must "work out [our] own salvation with fear and trembling," yet always remember that "God is at work in [us], both to will and to work for his good pleasure" (Phil. 2:12, 13). We must make full human efforts while believing that behind and around and beneath our efforts is God's controlling purpose accomplishing his eternal will in the unfolding pattern of our daily existence.

It doesn't make a whole lot of sense to believe that God created the world without also believing that God continues to provide for it. *Providence* is a word that identifies this continuing divine care. Providence includes not only those events that we judge to be good but also those that seem to be bad. God controls it all. According to the story in Genesis 37–50 Joseph had ten older brothers who didn't like him very much. They sold him as a slave into Egypt and for a while things went from bad to worse. Joseph seemed a forgotten man, abandoned by God and family. But eventually Joseph rose to great power in Egypt and became instrumental in saving both Egypt and its neighbors from starvation. Near the end of the story Joseph taught his brothers a lesson in God's providence. He said to them, "As for you, you meant evil against me; but God meant it for good, to bring it about that many people should be kept alive, as they are today."

God often works in mysterious ways. We don't understand why things happen as they do. But God the Father is moving the pieces of life's puzzle to produce the picture he has designed. There's comforting wisdom in the orchard conversation imagined by Elizabeth Cheney:

Said the Robin to the Sparrow:
"I should really like to know
Why these anxious human beings
Rush about and worry so."

Said the Sparrow to the Robin:
"Friend, I think that it must be
That they have no heavenly Father
Such as cares for you and me."

But we *do* have such a heavenly Father. Take comfort. God our Father created the vast universe and each small detail of life—he planned it all, made it all, rules over it all, and cares for it all.

The Covenant Father

The great Father God has chosen people to be his partners in arranging the affairs of his creation. God could have chosen other ways to deal with the world he had made. He could have acted the unpredictable tyrant—flashing out his commands, rewarding the obedient, destroying the rebels. Or he could have turned his creation into a massive puppet show, with each creature jerking automatically to a divine pull on the appropriate string. But God chose to deal with his world as a Father, calling his children into covenant with himself.

That's an important word in the faith and life of the Christian Reformed Church—*covenant.* Think of it as an agreement, except not an equal agreement. God established it. It was his idea. He set the terms. Still, even though the beginning of the covenant agreement lies with God, its continuing life embraces both God and people.

It's a staggering thought that the great God bound himself to the terms of his own covenant. It's like a mother and her son agreeing that the boy will sweep the basement and the mother will drive his team to Little League practice. The son is bound by covenant terms to sweep the basement floor; the mother is bound by the same terms to drive his team to practice. When the heavenly Father decided to deal with his people according to a covenant, he bound both his people and himself to the terms of that covenant. The covenant demands of us faith and obedience. But it also guarantees to us God's absolute faithfulness and trustworthiness. God will keep the terms of his covenant. He requires us to do the same.

The significance of that covenant theme becomes clearer if we trace it in Scripture. The first illustration of covenant is found in the opening scene of history. Genesis 1 and 2 tells us that God made human beings good and in his own image. Adam and Eve were without sin, fully capable of obeying God perfectly. God entered into covenant with them, binding himself to be their daily companion and binding them to obey him. For them obedience was the way of life, disobedience the way of death. Those were the covenant terms. God also gave Adam and Eve a beautiful garden to live in and required that they dress it and keep it, subdue it and have dominion over it. All of this was somehow sealed by the two trees in the garden—the tree of life and the tree of the knowledge of good and evil.

According to Genesis 3 Adam and Eve disobeyed God, failing to keep their side of the covenant. They were, therefore (according to the covenant terms), evicted from the garden and made subject to death.

Adam and Eve's sin in breaking covenant with God reached beyond themselves, for they represented all the human beings they would father and mother. When Adam sinned, all humanity sinned, and all were born sinners in a sinful world. The Canons of Dort explains the fallen situation simply: "Man after the fall begat children in his own likeness. A corrupt stock produced a corrupt offspring." As a result of Adam's sin, all people are born with a sinful nature. The psalmist confesses, "Behold, I was brought forth in iniquity, and in sin did my mother conceive me" (Ps. 51:5). Because of that sinful nature, we all sin; we do what we shouldn't do, and don't do what we should do. We don't glorify God as we should.

But that first sin of Adam and Eve and the continuing sinfulness of the human race did not change God's covenant posture. Adam and Eve had changed, but God had not. He was still the covenant Father. Therefore, even when he washed the rebellious world clean with the great flood (Gen. 7), he saved Noah and his family and reestablished his covenant with them. He promised never again to destroy the world with a flood and sealed that agreement by the sign of his rainbow in the sky.

Nowhere do God's covenant dealings with humanity come into clearer focus than in his relationship with Abraham. Unlike the covenant expressions with Adam and Noah (which included all human beings), God's covenant with Abraham called a separate community of believing people into special fellowship with himself. It was a covenant of God's gracious favor unto everlasting salvation. In the terms of this covenant, God bound himself to be faithful to all his promises and bound Abraham to believe, to "walk before me, and be blameless" (Gen. 17:1). God also made crystal clear that his agreement was not only with believing individuals but with their infant children as well. He made circumcision the sign of this covenant and promised Abraham's blessings to all who walked in Abraham's faith. The apostle Paul picked up that theme when he called all Christian believers children of Abraham, inheritors of the covenant promises that God first made to that father of all believers (Rom. 4:16-17, Gal. 3:6-29).

God's relationship with his people today, then, is part of that ancient covenant with Abraham. Old Testament Israel repeatedly broke their side of the covenant, but God never abandoned his side. According to the covenant terms, he punished his people when they disobeyed and forgave them when they repented. Finally he sent his own eternal Son to shed his "blood of the covenant" (Matt. 26:28) as an ultimate sacrifice for all who believe in Jesus. Covenant is the cloth on which God has woven the design of his fatherhood and the pattern by which he brought a people into partnership with himself.

The Covenant Translated

How is this teaching of God as covenant Father translated into the Christian Reformed Church's faith and life? Well, for one thing it's a tremendous comfort. If he is a covenant-making, covenant-keeping God, then his word is absolutely trustworthy. He has bound himself to the terms of the covenant he has made with his people. We can depend on that. Whether he speaks words of warning or promise, he speaks the covenant terms and those terms do not change.

Furthermore, as he binds his whole self to us in covenant, God also binds our whole selves to him. Living in our heavenly Father's family is no parttime experience, no merely mental or spiritual engagement limited to church worship or personal and family devotions. Our whole beings are embraced in covenant with God. Our whole selves must respond in faith, love, and obedience. Our whole lives are wrapped up in the covenant bond. That's why the Christian Reformed Church so frequently uses broad, inclusive phrases like "kingdom citizenship" or "a world and life view." Although we don't always give consistent evidence of such comprehensive living in God's family, we do believe that when he calls us into covenant with himself through faith in Jesus Christ, our Father lays claim to every square inch of our lives.

God as covenant Father also translates into certain distinctive patterns of attitude and behavior among us. Covenant consciousness prevents Christian Reformed Church people from seeing themselves as simply a collection of individual believers. To be sure each person must come to God through personal faith in Jesus Christ, but the covenant idea teaches us that the God who calls us into fellowship with himself does so in the context of a community of believers. It is in and through the covenant community that God calls us to faith in Christ and nurtures us in that faith.

Covenant has some very special implications for children born into Christian homes. Even before they know Jesus, they are members of God's covenant community. So it was with Abraham and his family, and the Bible gives no evidence that God ever changed his mind about including children in his covenant. Just as our children were born into one particular family and nation, so through believing parents they are born into the community of God's people.

Accordingly the Christian Reformed Church baptizes infant children of believing parents. They are baptized not because they've made a personal decision for Jesus, but because they have been born into God's family. And their baptism is God's public declaration that they are children of his covenant and must be set apart for a life of growing faith and obedient service. Baptism is not our human way of claiming salvation; it's rather God's way of saying that he extends all the promises and obligations of his covenant to children too. So children of believing parents grow up knowing that they bear the mark of God's covenant ownership.

One final note: the covenant teaching translates into what is sometimes called the "cultural mandate." Given to Adam, this mandate still applies to us. God said, "Subdue the earth. Have dominion over it." He gave us the earth to enjoy and use. He bound himself to govern the world according to the laws of nature he had created. He bound us to be good stewards of what he has entrusted to our care. The earth's resources, the farmer's produce, industry's output, the flow of human services—none of these are ours to use as we please. The universe is God's garden. We are God's gardeners.

The world belongs to our Father. That's wonderful! We are the Father's children. That's wonderful too! But most wonderful is the Father himself. Although at times we've abused his world, ignored his covenant demands, and doubted the certainty of his promises, he still loves us and calls us back into fellowship with himself through Jesus Christ. Our heavenly Father is so great that he can stoop to our weakness, rescue us from our sin, bring us into covenant with him, and set us on the road that leads to everlasting life.

We Believe in the Lord Jesus

Chapter
Five

Almost everybody believes that once upon a time a remarkable man named Jesus walked the earth. His mother, Mary, and his father, Joseph the carpenter, lived in the town of Nazareth in the land of Palestine. That's where Jesus grew up. When he became an adult, Jesus spent three years as a wandering teacher. Reportedly he was able to heal the sick and feed the hungry in miraculous ways. Yet in the very prime of his brief career he was executed by crucifixion. Later his friends claimed that he arose from the dead and ascended into heaven.

That much about Jesus everybody believes. It's part of the historical record. To deny that Jesus ever existed would be as foolish as denying the existence of Socrates, or Saint Augustine, or Joan of Arc.

But other things about Jesus aren't so easy to accept. Not everybody believes that Jesus was the Christ, the Son of God, our Savior and Lord. Not everybody believes that Jesus was born of a virgin or that he suffered, died, and rose again for our sakes. Not everybody believes that Jesus is now in heaven and that someday he will come to earth again. Not everybody believes these truths, but the Christian Reformed Church does. Why? Because the Bible tells us these things about Jesus.

We believe that Jesus is the Messiah, the Christ of God. The name *Christ* is the New Testament equivalent of the Old Testament title *Messiah.* Both mean "anointed"—that is, a person who is appointed to do a particular piece of work. Jesus is the Messiah–Christ, the one appointed by God to accomplish the work for our salvation.

Throughout the Old Testament centuries, God made it clear that someday that Messiah would come to do that work. Isaiah prophesied his birth: "Behold, a young woman shall conceive and bear a son" (7:14) who will be called "Mighty God, Everlasting Father" (9:6). Micah forecast that his birth would take place in Bethlehem (5:2), and Isaiah predicted that his life would not be an easy one. He would be "despised and rejected by men" (53:3) and they would make "his grave with the wicked" (53:9). It's impossible to read the Old Testament without catching some of the great expectation—that God would appoint someone to answer the most pressing needs of the troubled world.

And it's impossible to read the New Testament without recognizing that the one whom God appointed was the person known as Jesus of Nazareth. The apostle Peter had it right. According to the story in Matthew 16, Jesus asked his disciples, "Who do you say that I am?" Peter replied: "You are the Christ." In saying that, Peter was confessing that Jesus is the one whom God had promised—the Messiah, the Christ. The entirety of God's saving work and revelation is focused in Jesus Christ.

Jesus Is Lord

The heart of the Christian Reformed Church's confession about Jesus Christ is that he is Lord. The idea of lordship is not very familiar today. It comes from an earlier time, a time when vassals and slaves served their lords. Today the only human "lord" most people know is the landlord who collects the rent. Surprisingly that contemporary usage of the word lord can help us understand what "Jesus is Lord" means. The landlord owns the property. It is his. To confess that Jesus is Lord is to confess that he is the owner. The first question and answer of the Heidelberg Catechism says it this way:

> *What is your only comfort*
> *in life and in death?*
> That I am not my own,
> but belong—
>   body and soul,
>   in life and in death—
> to my faithful Savior Jesus Christ.

Jesus Christ is Lord. We belong to him. We are his property.

It's good when we are able to say honestly that Jesus is our Lord—Lord of our person, Lord of our family, Lord of our church, and Lord of our business. We find great peace and joy in knowing that Jesus owns every part of us. Instead of trying to control the issues of our lives, we surrender them to Jesus Christ.

But whether we confess Jesus as our Lord or not, the fact remains that he *is* Lord. Whether we acknowledge his ownership or not, he *is* the owner. Our act of honoring Jesus as Lord doesn't make him Lord. And bumper stickers that urge "Make Jesus Lord of your life" have missed an important truth. Jesus Christ *is* Lord. He himself made the startling claim, "All authority in heaven and on earth has been given to me" (Matt. 28:18). Jesus Christ, said Paul, "is head over all things" (Eph. 1:22); "he must reign" (1 Cor. 15:25). And when Thomas saw who Jesus really was, through the shadow of his doubt, he cried out, "My Lord and my God!" (John 20:28). It's no different with us. When we believingly and lovingly see Jesus as Lord, all we can do is worship him.

Take this confession that Jesus is Lord, blend it with a belief in the greatness of God, add the idea of covenant partnership and you have some of the ingredients that make up the characteristic faith attitudes of the Christian Reformed Church.

Parts of the Picture

The life and work of the Lord Jesus Christ is like a great mural woven into the background fabric of God's love for a sinful world. As soon as we stop to examine one part of the picture, we run the risk of losing the sweeping beauty of the entire mural. Yet it may be helpful to look more carefully at four parts of the biblical picture of Jesus: his birth, his sacrifice, his heavenly rule, and his second coming.

When we look at his birth, we see nothing lordly. He was born in the little town of Bethlehem. His mother was a peasant. His first visitors were shepherds. Nothing in the circumstances of his birth alerted the world to the birth of a great King. Yet on that first Christmas the Lord of heaven and earth came into human flesh. His birth is a miracle that staggers our imagination and challenges our faith. For when Jesus was born, God became man and yet remained God. We call this mystery the *incarnation*.

The Bible teaches that Jesus is true and eternal God, the second person of the Trinity. But in God's timetable Jesus became fully and completely human. The Gospel of John tells what happened simply and directly: in the beginning Jesus was with God and was God (1:1). Then this one who was God became flesh and came to live among us (1:14). As the angel told Joseph, Jesus was Immanuel, "God with us."

In his birth Jesus took our humanity upon himself. The true, eternal God became also true man. That didn't make him a split personality, sometimes acting like God and other times acting like a human being. He was not half human and half divine. Rather he was one complete and whole person with two complete and whole natures, one divine and one human. So he came to stand as the God–man between God and humanity, representing humanity in their sin before God and representing God in his justice and love before humanity.

The miracle of the incarnation happened through another miracle—the virgin birth. Scripture teaches that Jesus was like us in every way except that he was sinless (Heb. 4:15). Jesus had no sin of his own, nor did he inherit the sin of Adam and Eve as all other children do. How could that be? Only through God's intervention. There's no evidence in Scripture that Jesus' mother, Mary, was sinless. So for a naturally sinful mother to give birth to a sinless son, God had to intervene. As the angel explained to Mary, "The Holy Spirit will come upon you, and the power of the Most High will overshadow you; therefore the child to be born will be called holy, the Son of God" (Luke 1:35). By a supernatural act of God the virgin Mary became pregnant and the Lord of heaven and earth came into human flesh.

He was born. He lived. He died. He rose again from the dead. All of those events are part of the picture we call his *sacrifice*. Some look at this part of Jesus' life story and feel very sorry for him. Poor man! Meaning so well and yet so misunderstood. Ignored by his own neighbors, persecuted by the powerful, a victim of tragic circumstances far beyond his control. But that's not the Bible's picture.

The Bible teaches that Jesus was always Lord. Even in moments of deathly loneliness and lonely death, Jesus was in control. He was not sacrificed. He gave himself as the sacrifice. Jesus repeatedly testified to that: "I lay down my life for the sheep" (John 10:15), "The Son of man came to seek and to save the lost" (Luke 19:10), and "The Son of man came . . . to give his life as a ransom for many" (Mark 10:45). In the greatness of God's eternal love, Jesus Christ was a willing sacrifice.

Why was any sacrifice needed? To that the Christian Reformed Church answers by echoing the Bible's teaching: "to bear the punishment of sin" (Belgic Confession, Art. XX)—of *our* sin. He suffered and died for us, as our substitute, to pay for our sin and to satisfy God's holy justice. The sacrifice was for us—not in the sense that now we need not be born, live, suffer, or die, but in the sense that Jesus took on himself all our guilt that deserves God's judgment. To give an example, Jesus was like a divine vacuum cleaner, moving through each stage of human life from birth to death, drawing into himself the dirt of our sin and then removing it all by his sacrifice. His sacrifice was an act of immeasurable love which we can never fully understand, but for which we can be everlastingly grateful.

The Bible further teaches that Jesus' resurrection was also for us. When Jesus rose on the third day after his death, he broke the hold that death had on himself *and* on us. His bodily resurrection was God's declaration that the work of salvation was now completed and God's guarantee that the benefits Christ earned would now apply to all those who believe in him.

In the sacrament of the Lord's supper the Christian Reformed Church celebrates a mystery. The mystery includes the whole sacrificial work of the Christ who lives today. Somehow in the mystery of the sacrament, in a way we can't grasp, we participate in what Jesus has done for us. We eat and drink the benefits of his sacrifice. Somehow, through the sacrament, the risen Lord Jesus Christ lifts us into fellowship with himself.

Coming into a Christian Reformed worship service, you may find the celebration of the Lord's supper a rather somber affair. Although our souls sing with thankfulness for the enormous blessing of Jesus' sacrificial death, you may see little visible evidence of such joy. That's at least partly due to tradition and custom. But although it may often seem hidden, the victorious hope *is* present. We have hope because of Christ's sacrifice. And that sacrifice for our salvation is the centerpiece of the mural of his love and works woven on the fabric of God's love.

A third part of the picture is his *heavenly rule.* After Jesus rose from the dead, he stayed with his disciples for forty days. Then one day he took them up to the Mount of Olives beyond Bethany, spoke a few parting words, and then "was lifted up, and a cloud took him out of their sight" (Acts 1:9).

Why did Jesus ascend into heaven? One little six-year-old thought he knew the answer. After the story of Jesus' return to his Father's house had been retold in family devotions, the boy added his commentary: "Yeah, when Jesus finally got back to heaven, his Father said, 'You'd better stay up here now or you'll get into trouble again.' "

It's true that when Jesus ascended into heaven, that's where he stayed. That's where he is today. But he's there not to hide from the world's dangers but to continue carrying on the work that remains to be done. We confess in the Apostles' Creed that Jesus "ascended into heaven, and sitteth at the right hand of God the Father almighty." That means Jesus is now ruling all things according to God's great master plan. He's working for the final victory of his church. Jesus is in heaven now, preparing us by his Spirit for the final day of everlasting glory.

Hebrews 4 gives a most comforting picture of Jesus in heaven. It describes him as one who "in every respect has been tempted as we are" and as a result is able to "sympathize with our weaknesses." So "let us then with confidence," the writer urges, "draw near to the throne of grace, that we may receive mercy and find grace to help in time of need" (vv. 14–16). We have a voice in heaven, someone to speak on our behalf. He translates our feeblest whisper into a resounding request, worthy of God's attention. Our children understand this; that's why they pray confidently:

Jesus, tender Shepherd, hear me.
Bless thy little lamb tonight.
Through the darkness be thou near me,
Watch my sleep till morning light.

As surely as we know Jesus is in heaven answering such prayers, we also know he is *coming again.* The Bible leaves no doubt about that. Furthermore, although the mural of Christ's life and work is not yet completed, the outlines of his return are clearly drawn. It will be unexpected (Matt. 24:44), visible (Acts 1:11, Rev. 1:7), and glorious (Matt. 25:31, 2 Thess. 1:7). It will be preceded by many natural disasters and by human rebellion—the "birth pangs" of the end. All this will happen when God determines to bring down the curtain on our present history and usher in the perfection of his kingdom.

While all Christians agree that Jesus *is* coming again, they can't seem to agree how it will happen. Some of our brothers and sisters in other churches are deeply convinced that Christ's return will be in stages—a rapture, a millennium, and a final judgment. Others include two resurrections, a great tribulation, a loosing of Satan, and a battle of Armageddon. By such stages and elements they try to draw in the details to complete the mural.

But the Christian Reformed Church, looking closely at what the Scriptures say, does not believe it's possible to fill in all the details of Christ's return. We also do not believe that the Bible clearly teaches a rapture, a first resurrection, a thousand-year reign of Christ on earth, and then a second resurrection and judgment. And since we do not believe Scripture unmistakably draws that kind of millennial picture, we may not require such a belief as part of our Christian confession.

The Christian Reformed Church believes, as the Apostles' Creed confesses, that Jesus will come again "to judge the living and the dead." Four great events will mark that dramatic conclusion to world history: the Lord will return, the dead will be raised, the living will be changed, and judgment will be pronounced.

The Bible plainly teaches these four events. At the time of Christ's return, the dead will be raised from their graves (1 Cor. 15:22–23, 1 Thess. 4:16–17). People who are living at that time will be "changed in a moment, in the twinkling of an eye, at the last trumpet" (1 Cor. 15:51–52). And all will stand before the throne of divine judgment. "For we must all appear before the judgment seat of Christ, so that each one may receive good or evil, according to what he has done in the body" (2 Cor. 5:10).

That great day of the Lord is coming as certainly as tomorrow follows today. The same Christ who presides over life today will preside over that day of judgment. It is possible now to refuse to obey Jesus. But on that final day of history no one will be able to escape his judgment; it will be either "depart from me" or "enter into the joy of the Lord." Judgment then will depend on how we have responded to Jesus Christ now —with faith and obedience or with indifference and unbelief.

What will you do with Jesus?
Neutral you cannot be.
Someday your soul will be asking:
"What will he do with me?"

We Believe in the Holy Spirit

Chapter Six

He belonged to the religious separatists party. He was a member of its ruling body. His name was Nicodemus.

One night he came to visit Jesus. Their conversation soon turned to an enormously important question: how does one get into the kingdom of God? Jesus said, "You must be born anew." But Nicodemus didn't understand. Jesus explained, "You must be born of water and the Spirit." But Nicodemus still didn't understand. Jesus tried yet again, "That which is born of the flesh is flesh, and that which is born of the Spirit is spirit. Do not marvel that I said to you, 'You must be born anew.' The wind blows where it wills, and you hear the sound of it, but you do not know whence it comes or whither it goes; so it is with every one who is born of the Spirit" (John 3:6–8).

Nicodemus and the listening disciples probably still didn't understand Jesus' talk about water, wind, flesh, and Spirit—not until the day of Pentecost when "suddenly a sound came from heaven like the rush of a mighty wind, and it filled all the house where they were sitting . . . . And they were all filled with the Holy Spirit" (Acts 2:2, 4). When that happened, they understood. When that happened, Peter could explain that this was the coming of the Holy Spirit "upon all flesh" that had been prophesied in Joel. The sound of the wind, the tongues "as of fire," and the ability of the disciples to speak in other languages were all evidence of the Holy Spirit. This Holy Spirit, Peter said, had come to carry on the work and teachings of Jesus. He was the real presence of God in the church and in every believing heart. If people wanted to receive the Holy Spirit, said Peter, they must "repent, and be bap-

tized . . . in the name of Jesus Christ for the
forgiveness of [their] sins" (Acts 2:38).

The Holy Spirit and His Work

What does the Christian Reformed Church
believe about the Holy Spirit? First and
most important that the Holy Spirit is God.
He is not a lesser God; rather "he, as well as
the Father and the Son, is eternal God"
(Heidelberg Catechism, Lord's Day 20).

An interesting story in Acts 5 teaches the
divinity of the Holy Spirit. Ananias and his
wife, Sapphira, sold a piece of real estate
and made the grand and generous gesture
of giving the money they received for the
land to the church. The husband and wife
had watched other wealthy members of the
church make similar offerings and they
wanted their own little corner of praise and
congratulations. So they made a big show
of giving it *all*. Actually they had sticky
fingers: they kept part of the money for
themselves.

Now in itself that wasn't such a bad thing.
Likely no one would have thought less of
them if they had said, "Folks, we sold this
piece of property for $20,000. We plan to
keep $5,000 for ourselves and give the rest
to the Lord's work." But they didn't do that.
They pretended they had made the whole
sacrifice, and inside—as Peter said—they
had lied to the Holy Spirit. By doing this
they had lied to God because the Holy Spirit
is God. The story ends with the shocking
death of this couple—a divine judgment for
trying to deceive the Holy Spirit.

In the same breath with confessing that
the Holy Spirit is God, we also confess that
the Holy Spirit is a person, the third person
of the Trinity. Maybe the easiest way to
understand this is to say that the Holy Spirit
is not simply a power, a force. He's not "the

muscle in the arm of God" or a sort of divine dynamo into which we can plug for power. The Holy Spirit is personal. He has emotions, feelings, personality. He is happy when we live in love and obedience with God and grieved (Eph. 4:30) when we do not. The Holy Spirit is a person, as much a person as God the Father and God the Son. Thinking of the Holy Spirit, we must not think of an impersonal power but of a powerful person.

The Holy Spirit's work is far greater than we can catalog. As the person of the Trinity particularly responsible for putting into operation God's plan, the Holy Spirit is involved in all the work of God:

- He was operative in creation. "And the Spirit of God was moving over the face of the waters" (Gen. 1:2).
- He was active in the lives of the Old Testament people of God. David prayed, "Take not thy holy Spirit from me" (Ps. 51:11).
- He was responsible for Jesus' birth. The angel said to Mary, "The Holy Spirit will come upon you, and the power of the Most High will overshadow you" (Luke 1:35).
- He was present at Jesus' baptism. "The Spirit of God descended like a dove" (Matt. 3:16).
- He impelled the authors of the Bible to write as they did, guaranteeing its truth as God's Word. "Men moved by the Holy Spirit spoke from God" (2 Pet. 1:21).

The list of the Holy Spirit's work could go on and on. But as Jesus seemed to say to Nicodemus, the Holy Spirit's primary concern is to bring people to salvation in Jesus Christ.

The Holy Spirit does that in his own very personal way. He works within our hearts as the internal persuader. A little three-year-old, quite captivated with this thought of the Holy Spirit as God living and working in her heart, slipped her right hand inside her blouse and over her heart and said, "Yes, I can feel him bumping around in there."

The Means of Grace

The Holy Spirit doesn't work in our hearts without tools. He uses various means to awaken our interest in the gospel, to call us to repentance, and to build us in the faith. For example, he uses the same Scripture that he first inspired. He uses the preaching and teaching of God's Word. He uses the sacraments of the Christian church. He uses prayers, songs, worship, and a welcoming congregation. These are means, avenues, and tools the Holy Spirit uses to bring people to the Christian faith and to build people up in that faith.

In the Christian Reformed Church, we call these the "means of grace." It's important that people use the means of grace. To fail to go to church, study the Bible, and receive the sacraments—to ignore prayer, singing, and the fellowship of God's people in the worshiping congregation—is to take ourselves out of the very setting in which the Holy Spirit works.

To be sure, the Spirit can still find us in the corners where we try to hide from God. He's able to do God's work even in hearts that resist him. But we're responsible to go regularly to those gatherings and places where we're exposed to the means that the Holy Spirit uses for our salvation in Jesus Christ.

People's experiences of being saved and built up by the Holy Spirit vary greatly. Some are converted in a single, dramatic encounter with God. Others are slowly drawn with cords of love. The Bible itself illustrates such variety: the frightened Philippian jailer who urgently asked, "What must I do to be saved?" was converted that same night (Acts 16:30–34). Lydia was reached at an evangelistic meeting (Acts 16:11–15), and the Ethiopian eunuch through a theological discussion of a Bible book (Acts 8:26–38). Saul of Tarsus was converted on the Damascus Road by direct, divine intervention (Acts 9:1–9), while Timothy came to the Christian faith through Christian home training (2 Tim. 1:5, 3:15).

But in whatever way the Holy Spirit chooses to work salvation, certain elements are always present. There's always some kind of gospel invitation or call. "How are they to believe in him of whom they have never heard?" asked Paul (Rom. 10:14). There's also always the inner renewal by God's power that Jesus described as "being born again" and which we call *regeneration.* That makes it possible for us to hear the message of the gospel as God's word of love to us. Our response to that inner renewal is called *conversion*—our conscious decision to turn away from our sin to a life of obedience to the Lord Jesus Christ. After conversion ("being made right with God") we discover the blessings of our *justification*—the peace that comes from the assurance that for Jesus' sake God has restored us to his family. In Jesus Christ we are "no longer strangers and sojourners, but . . . fellow citizens with the saints and members of the household of God" (Eph. 2:19). What follows is a whole life of *sanctification,* of growing in love for the Lord and of doing his work on earth. In all of this the Holy Spirit is working around us, in us, and through us to accomplish God's purpose for us.

Special Gifts

The Christian Reformed Church emphasizes the person and work of the Holy Spirit, but not to the extent some Christians do. These others have been present in North America since the beginning of the twentieth century and are known usually as "Pentecostals," "Neo-Pentecostals," or "Charismatics."

The central teaching of Pentecostalism is that a "second baptism," a second receiving of the Holy Spirit, is needed to come to Christian maturity. By that, they mean a special spiritual (usually highly emotional) experience which occurs sometime after a person first turns to the Lord in faith.

Generally Pentecostals claim that the "gift of tongues" is the first evidence of such baptism in the Holy Spirit. Persons who are able to speak in tongues make sounds that neither they nor (normally) anyone else understands. Some call this tongue-speaking the language of the Holy Spirit or the language of heaven.

Another gift of the Spirit important to most Pentecostals is the miraculous ability to heal and to cast out evil spirits. Sickness is from the devil, they believe, so God wants all sick people to be healed. And he will heal them if only their faith is strong enough and the prayers of the believing community are fervent enough. Faith and prayer open the door for the Holy Spirit to give the gift of recovery.

There are some Charismatics within the Christian Reformed Church. Although we as a church are not Pentecostal or Charismatic, we do acknowledge Pentecostal Christians as our brothers and sisters in Christ. And we appreciate their strong emphasis on the Holy Spirit for it reminds us of a possible lack in our own teaching about the person and work of the Spirit of God.

Still we would lovingly remind Pentecostal Christians that the Holy Spirit is *one* person of a Trinity. No one person of the Holy Trinity may be made to overshadow the other two. As important as the Holy Spirit is, God the Father (with his work of creation and providence) and God the Son (with his sacrificial death and his living claim on our daily obedience) are no less important.

Furthermore, the special events so dominant in Pentecostal teaching do not stand at the center of God's revelation. Although there are Christians in the Bible who had a profoundly moving second spiritual experience, nowhere does Scripture assert that a second baptism is the God-willed pattern for every believer in Jesus. Although Paul mentions the gift of tongues, he also discourages any undue emphasis on its value (1 Cor. 14). And although Christians surely ought to believe that God can miraculously heal the sick, we may not make our faith and prayer conditions or guarantees of God's healing power.

Because the Charismatics try to make such exceptional and unusual biblical materials the pattern and experience for all Christians, the Christian Reformed Church takes a rather reserved position on the Charismatic movement. The whole focus of our faith is on God: Father, Son, and Holy Spirit. We adore God for what he has done, is doing, and will yet do. The focus of the Pentecostal faith, on the other hand, is on the way in which we experience the Holy Spirit. To Charismatics, special spiritual experiences can become more important than day-by-day living in the presence of God.

Yet, in spite of our reservations, we value some of the things the Charismatic movement has taught us. Their emphasis on the Holy Spirit has helped us rediscover what the Bible says about the gifts of the Spirit. Some Christians do seem to have received gifts of tongue-speaking, of healing, or of miracles. But those are only three of a much longer biblical list of gifts. God, through his Spirit, supplies each Christian with at least one gift, ability, or opportunity for service.

Paul says, "Now there are varieties of gifts, but the same Spirit; and there are varieties of service, but the same Lord; and there are varieties of working, but it is the same God who inspires them all in every one" (1 Cor. 12:4–6). Other biblical passages also make references to gifts (Rom. 12:6–8, 1 Cor. 12:28, Eph. 4:11, 1 Pet. 4: 10–11); teaching, service, helping, administration, giving, and evangelism are identified as just some of the many gifts that the Holy Spirit gives. Hebrews 2:4 summarizes the matter when it refers to "gifts of the Holy Spirit distributed according to his own will."

Careful study of the Bible has convinced members of the Christian Reformed Church that spiritual gifts are not given for personal enjoyment, but for building up the church. They are meant for the "common good" (1 Cor. 12:7), so that the church may be "edified" (1 Cor. 14:5) and, most clearly of all, "to equip the saints for the work of ministry, for building up the body of Christ" (Eph. 4:12).

Each church member's contribution may seem insignificant, but when each person called by God to the church of Jesus Christ contributes the gift provided by the Holy Spirit, we "grow up in every way into him who is the head, into Christ, from whom the whole body [the church], joined and knit together by every joint with which it is supplied [by the Holy Spirit], when each part is working properly, makes bodily growth and upbuilds itself in love" (Eph. 4:15–16).

The Christian character and attitude with which we receive and use the Spirit's gifts and which comes from the Spirit's power in our lives is described in the Bible as the fruit of the Spirit. The famous passage in Galatians reads, "But the fruit of the Spirit is love, joy, peace, patience, kindness, goodness, faithfulness, gentleness, self-control" (5:22–23). These are not nine conditions we must meet to win the approval of God, nor are they nine skills we must develop to be saved. They are rather nine virtues that occur in a life open to the Spirit's work. The fruit of the Spirit in our developing Christian character is evidence of the welcome that the Holy Spirit has found in our hearts.

And how do we welcome the Holy Spirit? We must ask God for his Spirit. Jesus once told a story about a boy who asked his father for good things, and the father gave such things to his son. Then Jesus added, "If you then, who are evil, know how to give good gifts to your children, how much more will the heavenly Father give the Holy Spirit to those who ask him!" (Luke 11:13). We must pray for the Holy Spirit. Or more accurately, we must pray that we become more aware and responsive to his presence and work in our lives.

But chiefly, the way to receive the Holy Spirit is to believe in Jesus Christ. The Bible never says, "Believe in the Holy Spirit and you will be saved." It rather rivets our attention on the Lord Jesus, his sacrifical death and victorious resurrection. The Bible says,

"Think on that! Believe that! It was done for you!"

And then, the strangest thing happens: the richer and deeper our faith in Jesus becomes, the more we become aware that someone other than ourselves is guiding, directing, moving us into the arms of God's love. That someone is the Holy Spirit. The faith that discovers Jesus as Savior and Lord also finds the Holy Spirit as God living in our heart. He is there as our Friend. He is there as our Companion. He is there as our Teacher and our Comforter. He is God, personally involved in our lives.

We thank him for being there and ask him to keep working to make us become what God wants us to be.

Our Church Fellowship

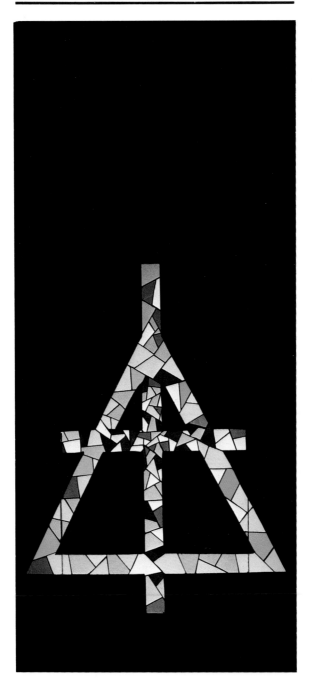

Chapter Seven

Once upon a time a man was hunting in a forest. When it started to rain, he looked for shelter but found only a hollow log lying on the ground. The fit was snug, but at least it was dry—so he crawled inside. It rained for hours, and the rain soaked into the wood of the log, swelling it with moisture. When the storm was over, the dismayed hunter found that he couldn't get out. He exhausted himself trying. Finally he gave up, convinced that he would starve to death. His life flashed before him. He recalled his past deeds, good and bad. He also remembered that he hadn't attended church as often as he should have. That thought made him feel small—so small, in fact, that he wriggled out of the log with no problem!

The story is a fable, slightly altered to introduce the subject of this chapter. What makes one "feel small" is the remembrance of something very important, neglected, something that should have been done before anything else, left undone. The story pictures the feelings many Christian Reformed people have about the church. Going to church is very important to most of our members. In fact, many visitors and newcomers are astonished at the common expectation that members will attend two worship services every Sunday.

And church attendance isn't the only important thing. The church's educational program, its mission to the world, its officebearers, its meetings, its finances, its concern for members' needs, its joy in members' successes—in short, the whole life of the church—are very important to Christian Reformed thinking.

The Church Described
Why is the church so important to us?

Because of the way the Bible describes it. In several places the Scriptures picture the church as the bride of Christ (Rev. 21:2, 22:17). This image conveys the idea that the Lord loves his church and rejoices when it shows love to him. Another biblical picture is that of a vine and its branches (John 15:1–5). Christ is the vine; the church is the branches, drawing life from him. Both of these descriptions (bride and branches) suggest an intimacy between Christ and his church—a dependence of the church on Christ, and a possessiveness of Christ toward his church. It's significant that Jesus is never recorded as saying "my home," "my donkey," "my coat," or "my money," but that he did say "my church" (Matt. 16:18). The church is so very important to Christian Reformed people because it is so important to Jesus Christ.

Another New Testament picture, the one most frequently used, reaffirms that importance. It's the picture of the church as a body of which Christ is the head: we, the church, are Christ's hands and feet and voice and heart in the midst of the world (see 1 Cor. 12:12–27). Just as there are many different parts in our human bodies, so there are many different members in the church. Just as some parts of our human bodies are more obvious and others parts less obvious, so in the church some members are more visible and others less visible. Just as in our human bodies each part needs the other parts to function properly, so in the church we need each other to adequately represent Christ in the world.

Thinking of the church in such biblical terms leads us to be very serious about that church. That's good. But that very seriousness has led Christian Reformed people to some extremes of which we're not proud.

Two extremes, in particular, result not from our indifference but from the very depth of our care for the church.

First, we get so wrapped up in the internal affairs of the church that we forget it's Christ's body in the world. As congregations we become at times ingrown. Such close friendships develop that, to an occasional visitor, the whole congregation may seem to be one big clique. We are grateful for that awareness of our interdependence, but we confess that, at times, our concern for each other has so occupied our attention that we have been insensitive to visitors and unresponsive to Christ's call to do his work in the world. For that failure, we repent.

Second, we've sometimes taken our responsibilities in the church so seriously that we've acted as if Jesus Christ himself was not able to take care of his church. We've been suspicious of new ideas, defensive in the face of criticism, protective of traditions (that have become like idols). We've stifled honest inquiry and loving disagreement. We're grateful for the passion that sets us on edge when we think there's a threat to the church's purity. But we confess the arrogant assumption that only our own wisdom will guarantee the church's future. That's wrong. The church and its future belong to Christ who declared: "I will build my church, and the powers of death shall not prevail against it" (Matt. 16:18).

The church, then, should not be a self-centered community whose purpose is its own self-perpetuation. It's not meant to be a country club for comfortable Christians. Nor is it meant to be a fort, built to keep the insiders in and the outsiders out. The church is a community of believers in Jesus Christ, ready to accept the risks of obeying him. It's an army, marching against evil to the victory already secured in the resurrection of Jesus. The church is the dynamic, self-sacrificing, discovering, loving, serving, obeying people of God on their pilgrimage to the heavenly city.

Our Church Order

Perhaps the best way to understand how Christian Reformed thinking about the church translates into practical church life is to follow the general outline of the Christian Reformed Church Order. This document introduces us to the offices, the assemblies, the activities, and the discipline of the church.

Offices: Most Christians agree that Christ rules the church by his Word and Spirit. But there is wide disagreement about how this takes place. On the basis of its study of Scripture, the Christian Reformed Church believes that Christ governs his church through four particular offices: minister, elder, deacon, and evangelist.

Ministers lead the church in public worship, preach and teach God's Word, counsel, and evangelize. Assuming that he has had the prescribed theological training and sanctions, a minister may become a pastor in a particular Christian Reformed congregation when that congregation votes to "call" (invite) him. A minister is free to "accept" or "decline" such a call.

Elders exercise spiritual supervision over the congregation's life. They are responsible to set priorities, maintain good order, develop new ministries, manage membership matters, exercise Christian care and discipline.

Deacons administer Christian mercy toward those in need. They have particular responsibilities for providing financial help and spiritual counsel to the sick, the poor, and the unemployed. Frequently, they've also been instrumental in resettling refugees.

Elders and deacons are elected from among the membership by a vote of the congregation. It's possible for a church to be without a minister for a short period of time, but every church always has elders and deacons.

Evangelists call unbelievers to the Christian faith. In general, they do the same things that ministers do, except that they usually work in developing churches and are assigned to work in some specific area.

These are four channels through which Christ ministers to his people so we call those who serve in these offices servants of Christ in the church. Although we believe that it is Christ's will to govern his church through these particular officebearers, we also believe that every believer bears the responsibility of all the offices. Each Christ-believing member of a congregation is to be like the minister in handling the Word of God, like the elders in guarding the spiritual life of the church, like the deacons in caring deeply for troubled people, like the evangelist in telling others the story of God's love in Jesus Christ.

Assemblies: The major forms of Protestant church government are usually called the Episcopalian, the Congregational, and the Presbyterian. The Christian Reformed Church operates under the Presbyterian system of church government. In this system there are at least three levels of assemblies where church business is conducted.

The first level is the local congregation and the officebearers it elects. In each congregation the minister, elders, and deacons are gathered into a consistory, council (or session). This is the basic governing unit of the church.

The second level is called the classis (like presbytery). This is a group of representatives from neighboring congregations. They meet together two or three times a year to deal with matters of common interest and to help individual churches with specific problems.

The third level is called the synod (like general assembly). This is a once-a-year meeting of representatives from all the classes of the Christian Reformed Church. Its purpose is to carry on the work of the denomination and to deal with issues that are properly presented to it by classes, consistories, and individuals.

Sometimes in the Presbyterian system of church government another level of assembly is introduced between the classis and the synod. This body is called a council of churches, or a particular synod.

The primary responsibility to govern the church according to God's Word lies with the local consistory. When the local consistory sends delegates to classis and when classis sends delegates to synod, they voluntarily place themselves under the authority of the broader assembly. By this action the consistory or classis binds itself to the decisions of the broader assembly unless it can show that those decisions are contrary to God's Word and the provisions of the Church Order.

Activities: The most obvious activity of the church is worship. Many Christian Reformed people have an attitude toward worship similar to that of an elderly British woman. Dreadfully crippled with arthritis, still she would hobble to church each Sunday supported by her two walking sticks. When asked how she managed it, she responded, "My heart gets there first, and my old legs follow on after." Almost all Christian Reformed churches place a like emphasis on public worship; the people rejoice in the enrichment it provides.

The Church Order reflects that commitment to public worship, although the appropriate article is more an invitation than a law: "The congregation shall assemble for worship at least twice on the Lord's day to hear God's Word, to receive the sacraments, to engage in praise and prayer, and to present gifts of gratitude" (Church Order, 51 a).

At least twice on the Lord's day! We can't demonstrate that God's Word requires a morning and an evening worship service each Sunday, but two services are a blessing to which we have bound ourselves in our Church Order. Although in a fragmented, pressured, mobile society it's become increasingly difficult to maintain peak attendance at both services, twice-a-Sunday worship is still one of the features of the Christian Reformed Church.

A second activity of the church is welcoming new members. Infant children of believing parents become members of the church through baptism. When these children grow older and come to an understanding of Christ and his church, they publicly profess their faith at a worship service and thus enter into communicant membership.

Others come to full membership by different paths. People who want to transfer to the Christian Reformed Church from some other denomination ask an officer of their previous church to send a statement of their baptism and membership status to the Christian Reformed congregation of their choice. These new members are often asked to attend a class of instruction. They may also be invited to make some appropriate public reaffirmation of their faith in Jesus. Recent converts to faith in Jesus Christ, people with no previous church home, become members through adult baptism (if they have never been baptized) or profession of faith. In either case their official entrance into the Christian Reformed Church is preceded by a period of instruction in the teachings of Scripture.

A third activity of the church is teaching children and young people "in order to prepare them to profess their faith publicly and to assume their Christian responsibilities in the church and in the world" (Church Order, Art. 63). Each Christian Reformed congregation is required to have church programs. When young people have been taught through this program and are ready to make public profession of their faith at a church worship service, they are first interviewed by the consistory. This interview is intended not to see how smart they are, nor to see whether they are proper graduates of a church school program, but to give them opportunity to testify to their faith in Jesus Christ.

A fourth activity of the church is pastoral care. Because the Bible teaches that the church is a body of interrelated members, the Christian Reformed Church takes seriously the requirement to "bear one another's burdens, and so fulfil the law of Christ" (Gal. 6:2). One concrete evidence of such pastoral care is called family visiting.

The Church Order requires the minister and elders to visit all congregational members in their homes on a regular basis. These visits are times to converse about personal, family, and congregational spiritual growth. Usually these are pleasant and rewarding visits. Sometimes needs and problems are expressed that would otherwise fester like poisons of dissatisfaction or doubt, infecting person, family, or congregation and destroying spiritual joy.

The last activity identified in the Church Order is missions. "In obedience to Christ's great commission, the church must bring the gospel to all men at home and abroad, in order to lead them into fellowship with Christ and his church. In fulfilling this mandate, each consistory shall stimulate the members of the congregation to be witnesses for Christ in word and deed, and to support the work of home and foreign missions by their interest, prayers, and gifts" (Church Order, Art. 73).

We Christians and our churches are not what Christ wants us to be unless we move out of ourselves and into our world with the gospel of God's love in Jesus. Worshipers leaving one of our buildings read these words boldly painted above the exit, "Your mission field is through these doors." Another Christian Reformed church has printed this motto on its weekly church bulletin: "Enter to worship. Go forth to serve."

Worship and evangelism are like two sides of one coin. We cannot do one without the other and still claim obedience to the Lord. In fact, all the activities of the church are of one piece. We worship, educate, welcome, care, and evangelize—all as part of being the body of Jesus Christ in the world.

Discipline: According to the story recorded in Genesis, Cain asked God, "Am I my brother's keeper?" (Gen. 4:9). Jesus in effect answered that question positively when he said,"If your brother sins against you, go and tell him his fault, between you and him alone" (Matt. 18:15). Eventually, continued Jesus, it may be necessary to report the matter to the church elders so that they may take appropriate action. But all church members are responsible to help their brothers and sisters along the road of Christian faith and obedience. That's always the purpose of Christian discipline in the life of the church—to help each other toward a closer walk with God.

The Christian Reformed Church takes church discipline very seriously. When members of the congregation sin openly and publicly, or grow indifferent to Christ and his church, the elders may impose restrictions against their membership privileges (such as forbidding them to take part in the Lord's supper). The elders may also ask the congregation to pray for a fellow member who is out of fellowship with Christ and the church. The elders may even, as a very last step, remove such a person from membership in the congregation.

But the whole disciplinary procedure is characterized by three words: patience, prayer, and penitence. Patience, because the elders move slowly, looking for even the slightest hint of the Spirit's changing a rebellious life. Prayer, because the elders know that it's only God's grace that will bring a wayward son or daughter back into congregational fellowship. Penitence, because the elders are painfully aware of their own sin, because discipline is applied only when there is no penitence, and because restoration to full congregational life follows swiftly the penitent's prayer, "Forgive, for Jesus' sake."

It's all part of that typically Christian Reformed understanding of the church as an interrelated body of people who need and are responsible for each other. That same understanding prevents us from having an "inactive membership role" where indifferent or hostile church members can gracefully hide. We expect all those whom God has called into our fellowship to participate fully in the community of God's people.

To participate means not only to join in loving the Lord and being part of his body, the church. It also means faithfully attending worship services and making certain that children are given instruction in the Christian faith. It means contributing time, prayers, money, and enthusiasm so that the church can do the work of Christ in the world. It means caring for others and being willing to be cared for by others. It means being part of a family, a family which, in the words of Robert Louis Stevenson, will continue to "live and love when the stars have passed away."

Our Pattern for Christian Living

Chapter Eight

Is it possible to let our conscience be our guide? Well, yes and no. Yes, in the sense that the Holy Spirit works through our conscience to direct us away from what is wrong: when our conscience troubles us over certain acts, we should stop them. No, in the sense that our conscience is an imperfect guide. It can be deceived and thus deceive us. Our conscience must itself be guided or shaped by God's Word. The Bible is always more authoritative than our own conscience. Our conscience can be our trustworthy guide only if it in turn is directed by Scripture.

Sometimes the Bible speaks clearly and precisely, telling us what is required and what is forbidden. When that's so, the correct Christian pattern is to obey. Many times, however, the Bible doesn't give us such precise directions, doesn't give a particular answer to a particular problem of Christian living. When that's so, the Christian's conscience, molded by the broad ethical principles of Scripture, must be our guide.

Our conscience, then, is one of the avenues that the Holy Spirit uses to pattern our lives in obedience to scriptural commands and in consistency with scriptural principles.

But molding our individual conscience according to Scripture is not left up to each of us individually. We should also be guided by a kind of community conscience. Take a junior high school student who sneaks a six-pack of beer in the bushes behind school to share with his friends. The teacher may be unable to prove from the Bible that such behavior is wrong. Furthermore, the student may claim that what he's done doesn't bother his conscience at all. This only means his individual conscience has not been instructed as it should be by a community conscience. Even though his own conscience may be untroubled, he should yet feel and respond to the restraints of the conscience of his family, his school, and his church.

The Christian Reformed Church has developed that kind of a community conscience which prescribes a pattern of Christian living. Anyone who really wishes to know about us should learn the values and styles of this denominational conscience. That's the purpose of this chapter—to give some insights into our church's conscience about the Christian life.

The Ten Commandments

A helpful way to learn the Christian Reformed Church's pattern of the Christian life is to see how we have come to interpret and use the Ten Commandments as our guide. Early in Israel's history God gave his covenant people the Decalogue (Ex. 20). Each of those Ten Commandments is repeated later, both in the Old Testament and the New Testament. They summarize moral law, a law intended to shape the conscience and lifestyle not only of Israel but also of God's covenant people today.

The first commandment—You shall have no other gods before me: A beautiful summary of how this commandment is meant to shape the Christian life is found in the Heidelberg Catechism. Question and Answer 94 states that in the first commandment the Lord requires "that I sincerely acknowledge the only true God, trust him alone, look to him for every good thing humbly and patiently, love him, fear him, and honor him with all my heart. In short, that I give up anything rather than go against his will in any way." At the beginning, at the end, and all along the journey of life the Lord God demands our total allegiance.

The second commandment—You shall not make for yourself a graven image: Images are really no problem in the Christian Reformed Church. On the contrary, we may try too hard to avoid the sort of artistic symbolism that could enrich our worship places.

But a first cousin to images is imagination. We are tempted to imagine what God is like, and then to limit our faith in him to our imagination of him. The result is that our God becomes too small. The second commandment tells us not to imagine God other than as he has revealed himself to us.

Surely, God has revealed himself to us in visible images—the beauty of nature and the physical presence of his Son during his earthly ministry. But God reveals himself to us essentially in the Word that we hear. Martin Luther once told a congregation, "If you want to see God, take your eyes and put them in your ears." That's a warning against trying to limit God to a visible image. It's also an invitation to know God and to worship him through the living preaching of his Word.

The third commandment—You shall not take the name of the Lord your God in vain: Ever since our birth in 1857, we've taken the position that a person can't be a member both of the Christian Reformed Church and of a masonic lodge, such as the Elks, Moose, or Eastern Star. One of the reasons for this rigorous position is our understanding of the third commandment.

To take God's name in vain is to use it irresponsibly and frivolously. Cursing and profanity are one example. But we also take God's name in vain when we use it to swear an oath that we really do not, or should not, mean.

To enter a masonic lodge, and to move from one level of its membership to another, a person is required to take a solemn oath to "never reveal any of the secret arts" of the lodge. Those taking such oaths bind themselves under such penalties as "having my throat cut from ear to ear, my tongue torn out by its roots and buried in the rough sands of the sea." Other oaths promise to have "my left breast torn open, my heart plucked from thence and given to the beasts of the field and the birds of the air as prey" and to have "my body severed in twain, my bowels torn from thence and burned to ashes and these scattered before the four winds of heaven." All these solemn words call upon God as witness: "So help me, God, and keep me steadfast."

A lodge member should never seriously make such terrible promises. These vows threaten suicide, and that's very wrong. But if a lodge member isn't serious about taking such required vows, then he shouldn't make them at all. A frivolous vow is taking God's name in vain.

That's one reason for the Christian Reformed Church's historic position on lodge membership. One can't systematically take God's name in vain as a lodge member and at the same time take seriously God's Word in the third commandment, "You shall not take the name of the Lord your God in vain."

The fourth commandment—Remember the sabbath day, to keep it holy: The rhythm of the weekly calendar is God's idea. Six days for work, one day for rest. Throughout the Old Testament that rest day was the seventh day of the week, Saturday. But since Jesus Christ rose on a Sunday morning so many years ago we, and almost all Christians, celebrate the first day of the week as that special day of rest.

The Christian Reformed Church has a sensitive conscience about "proper sabbath observance." Although practices of individual members vary widely, the community conscience of the church is committed to an entire Sunday kept very special. It should be a day for worshiping together in church, a day for families and friends, a day for physical rest and spiritual refreshment, a day for acts of kindness toward the needy. A nineteenth-century hymn describes it this way:

O day of rest and gladness,
O day of joy and light,
O balm of care and sadness,
Most beautiful, most bright.

The fifth commandment—Honor your father and your mother: By extension, this commandment also requires us to honor all those in proper positions of authority; "respect to whom respect is due, honor to whom honor is due" (Rom. 13:7).

But the commandment itself is essentially a family ordinance. Children are to honor their parents. The book of Proverbs tells children to pay attention to parental instruction. Ephesians requires children to obey their parents (6:1). Parents, in turn, are required to give good examples for their children to follow and are responsible to "teach them" (Deut. 6:7), to "train" them

(Prov. 22:6), and to "bring them up in the discipline and instruction of the Lord" (Eph. 6:4).

The Christian Reformed Church wears the fifth commandment comfortably. We eagerly accent the importance, value, and responsibilities of the Christian family because we believe that God has called such families into a covenant with himself, a covenant which catches them up into his everlasting family.

The sixth commandment—You shall not kill: The Christian Reformed Church understands this commandment to forbid not only murder but also a reckless lifestyle. The church has not banned smoking, drinking, eating too much, or driving too fast. But the conscience of the church teaches moderation in such things. Our bodies, says the Bible, are "temples of the Holy Spirit" (1 Cor. 6:19), and we may not, therefore, abuse or endanger them.

One official position of the church related to this commandment is its testimony on war. The Christian Reformed Church believes that a nation has the right to protect itself against invaders. The scriptural commandment that forbids killing does not seem to deny the duty of citizens to fight in their nation's defense.

But in a complicated world it's difficult to know with certainty whether a particular war is truly for self-defense. That's why, in its testimony on war drafted in 1939, the Christian Reformed Church allowed the possibility that some of its members might be conscientious objectors. An objector is a person with "intelligent and adequate grounds to be convinced that the given war to which he is summoned is an unjust war. When he is absolutely certain in the light of the principles of the Word of God that his country is fighting for a wrong cause, he cannot morally justify his participation in the given war. The only course open to such a person is to resort to passive resistance and to refuse to bear arms in that given war."

A second official position of the church related to the sixth commandment is its testimony on abortion. In 1971 our annual synod adopted three statements regarding induced abortion:

1. That synod affirm the unique value of all human life and the special relationship of man to God as his image-bearer.
2. That synod, mindful of the sixth commandment, condemn the wanton or arbitrary destruction of any human being at any state of its development from the point of conception to the point of death.
3. That synod affirm that an induced abortion is an allowable option only when the life of the prospective mother is genuinely threatened by the continuation of the pregnancy.

Synod went on to call upon the church to be compassionate and understanding of those with unwanted pregnancies and to help them discover alternatives to abortion. The Christian Reformed Church is one of those churches which has labeled abortion as killing.

A third official position of the church related to the sixth commandment is its 1981 testimony on capital punishment. The conscience of the Christian Reformed Church says that states do have the right to institute and exercise capital punishment, but that it is not a duty. In fact, when a state does practice capital punishment, it must do so with "utmost restraint and prudence."

Our sensitivity to the implications of the sixth commandment is rooted in our regard for God's gift of life.

The seventh commandment—You shall not commit adultery: The Christian Reformed Church has devoted a considerable amount of time and effort to studying what the Bible teaches about marriage, divorce, and remarriage. That study has left us deeply troubled over the prevalent marital breakdowns, divorces, easy remarriages, and subsequent new marital breakdowns.

We believe the Bible teaches that "marriage is intended to be permanent, to last until death terminates the relationship." Furthermore, since permanence in marriage is God's will, we believe God will enable us to sustain a marital relationship if we put our trust and confidence in him. "We do not possess within ourselves the power to keep the promise to be a husband or wife to the other and to love, honor, and cherish no matter what the circumstances of life, or what the other does to us or fails to do. Only the powerful grace of God can make each able" (1980 report).

Because God intends marriage to be permanent, there are no good, just, or justifying reasons for divorce. In a marriage-go-round world, it is still "the basic declaration of Scripture that divorce and remarriage while one's spouse is alive constitutes adultery" (Matt. 5:32, Mark 10:11–12, Rom. 7:2–3). The only exception Scripture allows is the unchastity or sexual unfaithfulness of one of the marriage partners. But even then the best solution is always repentance, forgiveness, and the rebuilding of a broken marriage. Marriage breakdown and divorce is a sin. It must be admitted as a sin and repented. Only God's forgiveness can give restoration and healing.

Homosexuality is another moral issue on which the Christian Reformed Church has taken a position. Based on careful Bible study, we have concluded that homosexual preference is no reason to exclude a person from the church, but homosexual practice is clearly condemned by Scripture. The following statement, one of eleven adopted in 1973, best reflects our position:

> The church must exercise the same patient understanding of and compassion for the homosexual in his sins as for all other sinners. The gospel of God's grace in Christ is to be proclaimed to him as the basis of his forgiveness, the power of his renewal, and the source of his strength to lead a sanctified life. As all Christians in their weaknesses, the homosexual must be admonished and encouraged not to allow himself to be defeated by lapses in chastity, but rather, to repent and thereafter to depend in fervent prayer upon the means of grace for power to withstand temptation.

In a supposedly sexually liberated society, the Lord calls his people to live in obedience to the seventh commandment and to seek by God's grace purity in thought, word, and deed.

The eighth commandment—You shall not steal: To steal means to take what does not rightly belong to us. Theft of all kinds is clearly wrong. But this commandment has deeper and wider applications. We rob God when we hold back from him our offerings for the support of his work (Mal. 3). We steal when we slander and gossip. Shakespeare wrote in his play *Othello*:

> He that filches from me my good name
> Robs me of that which not enriches him
> And makes me poor indeed.

The Christian Reformed Church stresses the positive side of the eighth commandment. The apostle Paul wrote, "Let the thief no longer steal, but rather let him labor, doing honest work with his hands, so that he may be able to give to those in need" (Eph. 4:28). Christian Reformed Church people are generally hard workers and generous givers, for we believe the eighth commandment requires this.

The ninth commandment—You shall not bear false witness: It's so easy to lie. The story of the evangelist who was conducting a series of nightly meetings illustrates this. One evening he announced that at the next meeting he would speak about liars. In preparation he asked the people to read Mark 17. The next evening he began by asking all those who had done as requested, who had read Mark 17, to raise their hands. About half the people did so. "Well," said the evangelist, "you're the people I'll be talking about this evening because there are only sixteen chapters in Mark's Gospel.

Cheating, lying, padding expense accounts, income tax dishonesty, exaggerated advertising, hypocrisy—all these are ugly evidences of sin forbidden in this commandment. God calls us to truth, for we follow the One who said of himself, "I am . . . the truth" (John 14:6).

The tenth commandment—You shall not covet: As the first commandment calls us in all of life to total allegiance to God, so the last commandment calls us in all circumstances to live with Christian contentment. Paul showed proper obedience to this word from God when he said, "I have learned, in whatever state I am, to be content" (Phil. 4:11).

This last commandment doesn't deny our striving, hoping, and dreaming. Rather it calls for a basic life attitude that says, "I live in God's hands. He knows exactly what he's doing. And his purposes are always good." That's the "godliness with contentment" which is a "great gain" (1 Tim. 6:6) because it emphasizes not the riches that we accumulate in this world, but the riches that we obtain through faith in Jesus Christ.

"In" But Not "Of"

The Ten Commandments and their implications have molded the conscience of the Christian Reformed Church. But the Bible has shaped our conscience in one other large area of Christian concern, what we call "worldliness." Scripture teaches that Christians are to live in the world but must not be identified with the world. They are to be *in* but not *of* the world.

It's impossible to list all of those worldly places and activities that Christians should avoid. In 1928, when the Christian Reformed Church first studied this issue, it put strictures on movies, dancing, and card playing as areas that illustrated worldliness. If the 1928 report were written today, perhaps the church would choose to speak instead against pornography, alcoholism, and gambling. At any rate, the point should be clear. There are places, activities, and circumstances from which God and his Word are obviously excluded; these are worldly things into which Christians should not enter. There are other places, activities, and circumstances where Christians can feel at home, for they can be there while being in the presence of their Savior, Lord, and Friend, Jesus Christ.

Christian Reformed people do not normally withdraw from the world. We are not other-worldly, detached from and uncaring about the events going on around us. But our conscience, trained by scriptural principles, tells us that while in the midst of the world, we belong to Jesus. In the world we must live for him.

The Bible tells us of a lawyer who tried to trick Jesus by asking him which was the greatest of God's commandments. Jesus answered with a one-word summary—love. He said: "You shall love the Lord your God with all your heart, and with all your soul, and with all your mind. This is the great and first commandment. And a second is like it, You shall love your neighbor as yourself. On these two commandments depend all the law and the prophets" (Matt. 22:37–40).

Love for God and for each other is the sum of what God requires of us. It is the one great summary principle which must bind the Christian's conscience and which must grace the Christian's life.

Our Mission to the World

Chapter
Nine

Have you ever stood on a high, rocky ledge and dropped a small stone into a quiet pond below? After the first splash, the water begins to ripple outward. Eventually, the ripples reach all the way to the edge of the pond.

The spread of the gospel is something like that. Jesus gave his church its marching orders, "Go therefore and make disciples of all nations, . . . in Jerusalem and in all Judea and Samaria and to the end of the earth" (Matt. 28:19, Acts 1:8). The good news of God's great love moved out like a series of ripples as the church dispersed into all the world.

Christians today continue to spread those ripples. Wherever the Lord places us, there we must show by example and tell by words that belonging to Jesus Christ is the greatest blessing in the world. Sometimes we bring that message as individuals. But other times, when our abilities and opportunities are too limiting, we band together in corporate action to bring the good news to the world.

Our Corporate Witness
The most obvious place where Christians work together to tell others about God's love is the local congregation. The advertised worship services themselves are part of the church's outreach. A friendly welcome, a reverent worship service, biblical preaching, and joyful singing are ways we witness to the goodness of God we've experienced as a local church.

We like to think that all our congregations are bundles of welcoming enthusiasm. But we know better. We've heard painful stories of people who wanted to know God better—until they visited a church. There they found the welcome cool, the worshipers restless, the sermon dull, the singing joyless. The entire experience was singularly unattractive. We're sorry when that happens.

An entirely different experience that may discourage visitors is our practice of "supervised communion." Suppose a stranger visits a Christian Reformed Church on a Sunday when the Lord's supper is celebrated. An elder at the door may ask some pointed questions about why this visitor desires to partake of the sacrament, whether she loves the Lord and what her church membership is. Or an usher may ask the visitor to sign a card requesting permission to share in the sacrament. Or there may be a carefully worded invitation from the pulpit. At any rate, the screening process may be enough to discourage the visitor from ever coming back again.

We can understand that reaction. But we hope that our custom of supervised communion is never seen as a barrier to people who wish to worship with us. We hope it is seen rather as a testimony to our serious regard for the sacrament of Christ's sacrificial death. While we certainly don't wish to limit the Lord's supper to Christian Reformed Church members, we don't feel right about opening it to everybody. We want to welcome all who love the Lord and his church. But the sacredness of the sacrament requires the church's spiritual leaders to make sure that all who participate are known to be believers in Jesus Christ and members of his church.

Properly understood, even supervised communion can be part of a church's welcoming warmth. We are a church that takes Christ and the fellowship of his faith seriously. And any church that's serious about Christ and the faith is a church worth taking seriously.

In addition to inviting people to worship services, most Christian Reformed congregations have some organized effort to bring the gospel to their communities in word and deed. Such efforts may include conducting a Vacation Bible School; visiting nursing homes, hospitals, and jails; calling door to door; distributing Bibles and tracts; and organizing Bible study clubs. Some churches broadcast on radio or television. Others engage in a wide range of social ministries to the needy. Like that pebble thrown into a quiet pond, so the outreach activity of a church spreads throughout its community.

Funding the Mission

Much of this work of corporate Christian outreach doesn't need any financial support. It's simply willing work of loving volunteers. But the church and its outreach programs do need financing. To provide that, the typical Christian Reformed Church adopts a budget at its annual congregational meeting. The people then give pledges to meet the budget upon which they have agreed.

Part of each annual congregational budget is designated for what is called "Classical and Synodical Quotas." These are amounts of money agreed upon by representatives of the church meeting in classis and synod. Classical quotas are used to support work that churches in a given area are doing together. Synodical quotas are used to support work that the entire denomination is doing. Through these quotas each congregation participates in the whole denominational effort to extend the ripples of the gospel message to the ends of the earth.

By far the biggest section of the quota goes for missions. In some areas a classis or group of churches sponsors a church planting or other outreach project. The Canadian churches, for example, have their own mission work among native Canadians in Winnipeg and Regina. But the Christian Reformed Church does much of its mission work through its denominational program, supervised by a Board of Home Missions and a Board of World Ministries.

The Board of Home Missions administers an ambitious program of church planting in Canada and the United States. It also advises and assists local congregations in their own evangelistic work and engages in specialized ministries to college and university students, to those in the armed services, and to seamen in several major North American harbors. One of Home Missions' largest evangelism programs is located in Southwestern United States among the native Americans.

The Board of World Ministries, composed of the Christian Reformed World Missions Committee and the Christian Reformed World Relief Committee (CRWRC), circles the globe with its work. World Missions has located major concentrations of Christian Reformed missionaries in Nigeria, Japan, the Philippines, Argentina, and Central America. Some of those missionaries are church planters; others are teachers in Bible schools and seminaries. Some are pilots and mechanics, some preachers, some doctors and nurses. All are busy in the work Christ gave his church when he told it to go out into all the world.

When Jesus sent his disciples out to do his work in their communities, he gave them these orders: "Preach as you go, saying, 'The kingdom of heaven is at hand.' Heal the sick, raise the dead, cleanse lepers, cast out demons" (Matt. 10:7–8). The "preaching the gospel of the kingdom" part of Jesus' instructions is the work of our Home and World Missions. Much of the remainder, meeting the physical needs of people, is the mission of CRWRC. In the name of Christ this organization responds to disasters like hurricanes and earthquakes. It has also developed relief programs in Southeast Asia, Africa, Latin America, and in various North American localities where there is critical human need. In addition to its disaster response and its relief programs, the CRWRC carries on an educational program to teach us about problems like world hunger and what we can do about them. The CRWRC is supported not by quota funds but by generous love offerings from the people of God.

The Back to God Hour, another agency funded through quotas, is a radio and television ministry of the Christian Reformed Church which preaches the Word of God and distributes evangelistic materials in English, Arabic, Spanish, Chinese, French, Indonesian, Japanese, Portuguese, and Russian. The Christian Reformed Church is grateful to God for this mission of denominational broadcasting he has granted us.

Each year a large part of denominational quota goes to Calvin College and Seminary. Although a seminary is necessary for church life, a liberal arts college may not seem a necessary part of the church's outreach activity. But Calvin College and its sister colleges in the United States and Canada (Dordt College, Trinity Christian College, The King's College, Redeemer Col-

113

lege, and Reformed Bible College) are part of the Christian Reformed vision of a world under the lordship of Jesus Christ. Not all graduates of our colleges carry the gospel to the mission field, but they do carry into various areas of life a testimony to Christ's authority over every life activity.

Through quota contributions, every local congregation is involved in that whole array of denominational work. In this way each member takes part in the church's work as it reaches into all the world.

But that's not the whole story. Many congregations contribute more than the quota amount for denominational work. Without those "above-quota gifts" the work of denominational outreach could not be nearly as ambitious as it is. Through giving a promised percent of income, or through a Faith Promise program, or through special offerings, Christian Reformed congregations share the excitement of giving an extra measure for God's work in the world.

Citizens of God's Kingdom

The work of missions is uniquely the church's work. But Christians are not only church members. We are also citizens of something bigger than the church—God's kingdom. And we join together with other Christians doing kingdom work in hospitals, health care centers, agencies to help the disabled, and Bible and tract distribution. Perhaps the biggest kingdom task which Christian Reformed people enthusiastically support is Christian day school education.

From the beginning of its history the Christian Reformed Church has encouraged the establishment of Christian day schools. The Synod of 1898 stated one reason for this: "There may be no separation between civil, social, and religious life, education and training." The Christian Reformed Church has always insisted that a person cannot be divided into a secular and a sacred part, with the church concerned only about the sacred part. Our whole selves must be trained in and brought under the authority of God's Word. The Synod of 1955 reaffirmed that position: "A dualistic view of education which calls some education religious and other secular fails to grasp that . . . in all our ways we are called upon to acknowledge God. Man is an organic whole. To bring all faculties into spiritual service and to bring all of life's activities under the discipline of God's will, education should be of one piece in which a person's earthly relations and functions, as well as his relations to heaven, are centered in and directed by the standard of God's Word." The Christian Reformed Church has translated that position into vigorous support for a Christian school system.

Christian schools are not "pin the tail on the donkey" copies of public schools. In other words, we don't take the public school curriculum and simply "pin" a Bible course and a weekly chapel on it. Good Christian education, as we see it, brings the student face to face with God's overwhelming greatness and Christ's claim to ownership of both our world and our lives. And that face-to-face experience happens in history and algebra as well as in Bible and chapel.

We think that's important. So we continue to support Christian schools even though it's an expensive commitment. Many Christian Reformed people carry a sort of double burden. They support the public school system through taxes and the Christian schools through tuition and contributions. But even under such burdens our commitment to Christian schools is sustained by our belief that Christian education is God's will for the nurture of our children.

We also believe it is God's will that we speak unitedly on economic, political, and social issues. In 1883 we questioned a Christian's role in a non-Christian labor union. Out of our studies and discussions a Christian Labor Association was formed and became in some places a significant force for good. Even where a Christian Labor Association didn't emerge, people developed a deepened awareness of our Christian responsibility to live as Christ's disciples, both on the job and in the union hall.

Although we haven't organized political and social parties, we have formulated positions on political and social issues. We feel compelled to witness as Christians also in the public arena. We're not always as courageous as we'd like to be. Our voice isn't always as clear as it should be. But we treasure the vision of being Christ's people who voice Christ's claim over the world—"You are mine."

Jesus told a story that challenges us to keep that vision alive (Matt. 25:14–30). Once upon a time there was a businessman who had to leave for an indefinite period of time. Rather than sell his business, he called three employees into his office and gave each a particular responsibility over his affairs. Then he left. Two of the three took the entrusted tasks seriously, diligently developing their part of the business. But one of the employees did almost nothing. He kept his part of the business going, but did nothing to develop it.

Eventually the businessman returned. Two employees turned back their share of the business with a good profit. The third employee returned to the businessman exactly what he had received. The businessman was so upset over the last employee's lack of diligence that he fired him on the spot.

This story tells us something of the Lord's wishes about his work in the world while he's gone. He has entrusted the Christian Reformed Church with part of his business. We are to take the teaching, heritage, abilities, and opportunities he has given us and use these to promote his work in the world. Someday the Lord will return. We will have failed miserably if all we can do on that day is return to him what he first gave us. We've been instructed to reach ever further into the world with the gospel of God's love. The Christian Reformed Church is trying to be obedient to that command of Christ.

But our mission to the world is born out of more than obedience. It comes also from compassion. So much in the world reveals human sin and the destruction that follows in its wake. So much begs for the healing mercies of Jesus Christ and the saving message of his gospel. We can't do everything, but we want to do something to touch the aching wounds of poverty, hunger, injustice, and disaster. We want to do everything we can to tell the world "Jesus saves!" Believing in Jesus Christ is finally the only hope for a broken world.

We want to obey Christ's command. We feel sympathy for a suffering world. But our mission to the world is born out of one more element—dissatisfaction. We're incomplete. We need others. We don't need them to fill empty pews, to pay bills, or to bolster our growth statistics. We need others because our joy is incomplete until others enjoy it with us. Like our delight in a beautiful picture or a newborn child, the joy isn't really full until it's spilled over into the lives of others. Joy is meant to be told.

That's why we're dissatisfied. Some people are still strangers to the joy of salvation. They, too, must be told. Until the Lord comes again, that is the church's business.

Jesus himself prayed for the success of this work. On the eve of his crucifixion he not only prayed for the unity, safety, and growth of the church but also for the success of its mission to the world (John 17). This is a prayer Jesus himself is now answering from his place of heavenly authority where he rules "all things for the church, which is his body" (Eph. 1:22–23).

The Christian Reformed Church is part of that great body of people whom the triune God has embraced in his love. In grateful response, we accept our high calling to live by God's saving grace under the sovereign lordship of Jesus Christ.

To God be the glory, both now and forever. Amen.

For further information about the Christian Reformed Church, contact a local Christian Reformed congregation or one of the following agencies:

The Back to God Hour of the Christian Reformed Church
6555 W. College Drive
Palos Heights, IL 60463
phone (312) 371-8700

The Board of Home Missions of the Christian Reformed Church
2850 Kalamazoo Ave. SE
Grand Rapids, MI 49560
phone (616) 241-1691

The Education Department of the Christian Reformed Church
2850 Kalamazoo Ave. SE
Grand Rapids, MI 49560
phone (616) 241-1691

These agencies may also be contacted through the Canadian office:

760 Brant St., Suite 408
P.O. Box 5070
Burlington, ON L7R 3Y8
phone (416) 637-3434